20 Dictators of the World

20 Dictators of the World

Kalyani Mookherji

Ocean Books Pvt. Ltd.
ISO 9001:2015 Publishers

Published by
Ocean Books (P) Ltd.
4/19 Asaf Ali Road,
New Delhi-110 002 (INDIA)
e-mail: info@oceanbooks.in

ISBN 978-81-8430-369-8
20 DICTATORS OF THE WORLD
by Kalyani Mookherji

Edition
2025

Price
₹ 300.00 (Rupees Three Hundred only)

Printed at
Narula Printers, Delhi

Introduction

Ever since humans started living in societies, there has been some system of governance. The complex process of cooperation, compromise and threat that a social group is based upon, needs a leader to make rules and enforce them, so that the group functions as a whole.

In the twentieth century, due to a combination of political and historical factors, two main types of governments came to exist in most parts of the world – democratic and autocratic. In case of the former, the government was run by elected representatives of people to whom it was ultimately accountable. In an autocracy, an individual exercised absolute authority, without being accountable to anybody.

Autocratic system of governance was nothing new. The monarchy, the most common form of governance in earlier times, itself was an autocratic system in which power resided in the king or monarch. Eventually, in the late nineteenth and twentieth century, with the disappearance of monarchies in many parts of the world, a new autocratic system emerged – the dictatorship, in which all power over a state or community was again concentrated into the hands of one person, without being restricted by constitution, laws or opposition. The individual with this kind of absolute authority was known as the dictator.

But there was an important difference between a monarch and dictator. While in case of the former, the authority was naturally invested in the royal lineage, a dictator often turned out to be self-made. Many dictators of modern history emerged from humble backgrounds and by dint of military service or political activism, ascended to the most powerful position in the country.

Another interesting trait about dictators from the modern history has been that many of them came to the power on the strength of the same institution – democracy – that they eventually subverted in the process of establishing their absolute authorities. Thus, dictators like Adolph Hitler and allied parties which actually did well in elections.

More often though, dictators rose to the power by leading a coup détat, in which often a weak monarch of government was deposed and instead a dictatorship established.

Sometimes again a dictator's rise to power was paved by an autocratic system of government in the country – the Soviet Union for example, has established such kind of government in which the Communist Party was supreme and there was no opposition party. Hence, any leader who held the reins of the party in his hands, like Stalin and later Brezhnev, emerged with dictatorial powers.

Here are the twenty dictators of modern times whose actions have left a strong imprint on destiny of the country they ruled, and sometimes even influenced the very history of the world.

—Kalyani Mookherji

Contents

Porfirio Diaz

D.O.B. – 14th Sept., 1830 Country – Mexico
D.O.D. – 2nd July, 1915

Porfirio Diaz was a Mexican military general, who went on to become the President of the country and remained in power for three and a half decades. During this time, known as the *Porfiriato,* he transformed Mexico into one of the most developed economies of Latin America but later came under criticism for centralizing the authority and concentrating power into his own hands.

Early Years

Belonging to a *mestizo,* or mixed Indian-European heritage, Diaz was born in the state of Oaxaca in 1830. His father, a humble innkeeper died, when Diaz was just an infant. Modest circumstances of his family could not afford to give him a regular education. He, thus, began his training for priesthood at an early age and his mother sent him to a Catholic seminary.

However around this time, Diaz was influenced by the liberal politics and work of the Mexican leader and President, Benito Juarez and, thus, decided to study law for which he enrolled at the Instituto de Ciencias. But Diaz was not satisfied with the legal career and while he was considering what to do in life, the war broke out between Mexico and the United States in 1846. Diaz immediately joined the army. Later, he joined a guerilla group who were fighting against the forces of Mexican General Antonio Lopez de Santa Anna.

By this time, Diaz had realized that his true place was in the military and he decided to make a career out of it. He proved his worth as a soldier and then military leader in the Reform War, which centred on an extended struggle between Liberal and Conservative forces in Mexican politics that played out for most of the 19th century.

Rise to Power

However, it was really in the fight against the French forces that Diaz rose as a military leader of great potential. The Battle of Puebla was especially significant in this context. On May 5, 1862, the Mexican General Ignacio Zaragoza led his soldiers against a French army outside the city of Puebla. Though the invading French forces were greater in number and better equipped too, they were defeated by the Mexicans. One of the foremost reasons for the Mexican victory was the leadership and personal bravery displayed by the young Diaz, who was a young commander of a cavalry unit at that time. Though eventually the French forces rallied back and later seized control of the capital city, the Battle of Pueblo made Diaz famous across the country as a military hero and marked him as a leader of the future.

Another consequence of these military engagements was that it afforded Diaz an opportunity to serve under his political hero, Benito Juarez even though the relationship between them never turned personal. During the three year rule of Maximilian of Austria, Diaz still offered his services to the Liberal forces. In the elections of 1871, he ran against Juarez. Diaz lost in the elections and even started an insurrection which took Juarez no less than four months to suppress.

1872 however marked a turning point in the history of Mexico. Benito Juarez died suddenly and the resulting political vacuum paved the way for conflict among various leaders eager to form the government. Eventually, it was Diaz who succeeded with substantial help from the United States as well as the Catholic Church, which was quite influential in Mexico. In 1876, Diaz led his army into Mexico City and virtually staged a coup. Then President Sebastian Lerdo de Tejada was removed from power and an election ordered which eventually turned out to be an eyewash, performed mainly with the intention of enabling Diaz to form the government. On 12 May 1877, Diaz was elected President of Mexico for the first time and he went on to rule the country with an iron hand for the next thirty-five years, with the brief exception of four years from 1880 to 1884, when he ruled through proxy during the Presidency of Manuel Gonzalez.

Political Power

Diaz was able to concentrate power in his hands for such a long period with a cunning mix of patronage and fear. To his allies, he would grant favours and rewards, while his opponents would be threatened with violence and death. Another way that Diaz retained control was by keeping all the stakeholders of Mexican Government in tight control. He never allowed any particular section of the society – be it the rich landlords or the Church – to amass too much power. For example, competing sections like the Mestizos as well as the wealthier indigenous people, were given influential political positions. With respect to the elite Creole society, he adopted a policy of non-interference and let them enjoy their money and haciendas. Likewise, with religious institutions for example, Diaz was at the same time the head of the Freemasons in Mexico as well as chief advisor to the Catholic Church. In this way, Diaz would distribute just enough favours among all sections to retain their allegiance but he never favoured so much as to make them more powerful than him.

The absence of true democracy was in fact reflected on one of his favourite maxims – "little of politics and plenty of administration". An extreme centralization of government became the hallmark of the Porfirio period. Through a combination of coercion and manipulation, Diaz dismantled the federal structure of the government and dissolved all local power centres. All kinds of administrative heads were directly accountable to him and after a while, even the press and judiciary were brought under his indirect control.

Though this kind of strict centralization of power brought about internal stability, but at the cost of large-scale violation of human rights as well as the health of democracy. From the very start, he manipulated elections to give himself the edge over his political opponents. His supporters also launched the No Re-election Campaign according to which no political opponent was allowed to claim fraud in the election and demand a re-election.

Once Diaz finished his first term of Presidency, he installed the puppet government of Manuel Gonzalez. Latter became so infamous for ineptitude and corruption, that people brought Diaz back to power with almost relief, little realizing that all along he had the reins of the government in his own hands. After Diaz came back to power the second time, Diaz used his influence over the legislature to amend the Constitution so that he could continue as the President for successive terms. In this way, Diaz for over three and a half decades manipulated every arm of the government – the legislature, judiciary and executive – to continue as the absolute ruler of Mexico.

Economic Reforms

Though Diaz was confident of his absolute rule over Mexico, he also realized that without generation of wealth, he would not be able to continue his hold over different sections of the society for long. As such, he initiated several reforms to accelerate the growth of the Mexican economy. At the centre of this was his plan to attract foreign investment in the Mexican mining sector. With the help of tax waivers and other incentives, Diaz motivated investors to put in money and consequently helped jumpstart economic growth. While the Americans and British investors were attracted to the mining and energy sector, the French controlled textile factories and the Germans dominated the drug and hardware industries. Likewise, merchants and workers from Spain sought to take advantage of economic opportunities in Mexico and flocked to its cities and plantations. This infusion of capital and labour proved beneficial for Mexico's economy and its cities. For instance, the commercial development of the El Boleo copper mine not only led to growth of towns like Santa Rosalia but also helped in the development of hitherto-neglected regions like Baja California Sur. Likewise, local silver mining ventures, led to the revitalization of cities like Guanajuato. The inflow of foreign investment made these cities prosperous which was exemplified by the construction of several landmark buildings, like the magnificent Juarez Theatre in Guanajuato.

On the flip side, these economic measures benefited only the elite sections of Mexican society. Those who already owned farms, industries and mines became even wealthier while the poor rural masses found themselves dispossessed of whatever little they had owned till now. For instance, Diaz ordered the privatization of communal indigenous landholdings which were then subdivided and sold to other classes. Thus, the rich got richer while the poor became even more impoverished.

Besides leading to growing disparity between the haves and have-nots, the economic measures initiated by Diaz were also responsible for entrenching unequal regional development in Mexico. Thus, the northern part of the country became famous for its wealthy ranches and profitable mines while the most of the grain farms and industrial centres were located in the central valley.

Though some kind of economic progress came to all regions, the degree of benefit varied widely just as the lack of diversification brought its own problems:

Later Years

Despite all efforts by Diaz to retain complete control over Mexico, his rule seemed to slacken from the beginning of the twentieth century. The initial burst of economic prosperity brought on by reforms was over and now problems started showing up, which was heralded by the onset of economic recession.

Secondly, decades of economic disparity was bound to have its effect. The miners finally took to protesting against harsh working and living conditions while the mine owners and industrialists took home all the profits.

Finally, the expatriate Mexican community played an important role in expressing the latent dissent against Diaz's rule. A large number of Mexicans who had fled his dictatorial system had taken refuge in Southern United States. They now started gathering public opinion against Diaz's government through various means like publications in press as well as lectures or meetings. Even at home, Diaz's own supporters began to get uneasy at the lack of any clear rule of succession and wondered what would happen after his death.

Diaz became aware of all the speculation surrounding him and in a bid to put fears to rest, in 1910, he announced that Mexico would soon hold free and fair elections. After decades of absolute authority, Diaz believed that no one could shake his power and that even if elections took place, he would still win a majority. However, Diaz failed to notice the desire for change that had started blowing in Mexico. And leading the challenge against him a writer and spiritualist from the country's elite class, Francisco I. Madero. Though Madero had no great leadership skills or personal charisma, he believed that the time had come for

Mexico to see a change in government and that he was well placed to use that opportunity.

However, when the elections took place, Diaz was taken aback by the votes polled in favour of Madero and immediately fell back upon his old strategy of rigging the elections and declaring himself the winner. After a brief period of arrest, Madero was freed but he fled to the United States where he announced the elections a fraud and called for an armed revolution against Diaz. This paved the way for the Mexican Revolution which ended the three and a half decade Porfiriat and plunged the country into a ten year long civil war, finally ending around 1920.

One of the most important factors responsible for Diaz's downfall was the support of the poor across the country, who had been victims of the worst effects of the economic reforms. Dispossessed of all political rights and exploited by rich landowners, industrialist and mine owners, the poor had suffered for decades and were seething in anger. In the military too, there was great discontent in the lower levels. Though the officers had been well looked after by Diaz, the ordinary soldiers were ill-paid and badly treated.

Conditions were thus ripe for a revolution and in different places of the country, rebel leaders began harnessing the discontent of the people. In the north, rural warlords, Pancho Villa and Pascual Orozco amassed men and weapons to carry out guerilla warfare against the government force. From Morelos emerged Emiliano Zapata, who had been opposing the oppression of wealthy landowners for more than a year and now saw an ally in Madero. Gradually, the rebel forces began increasing their control over Mexico till they were poised to take over the capital city. At last in May 1911, Diaz was compelled to cede control of the government and was left the country for Spain. He lived out the rest of his days in exile and died in Paris on 2 July 1915.

Legacy

Porfirio Diaz remains one of the foremost figures of post-independence Mexican history. He however left behind a mixed legacy and his thirty-five year rule has been both praised and criticized by historians and later generations of Mexicans.

On the plus side, he ushered in a long era of political stability in the country, which led to important gains for the economy and administration. When Diaz seized power in 1876, Mexico had been ravaged by decades of international and domestic conflict. The economy was in shambles and still seemed stuck in medieval ages. For example, at the time—there were just five hundred miles of railway tracks in the whole of the country. The nation was run by a handful of regional leaders who often bickered amongst themselves and were answerable to none.

With Diaz taking over the reins of the country, the regional power centres were demolished and replaced by a strong centralized government. This iron grip resulted in long era of political stability, which in turn encouraged foreign investment so that Mexico soon saw rapid economic growth, driven by the mining and industrial sectors. The country that Diaz had taken over in 1876 had now given way to a Mexico that was completely different and ready for the twentieth century.

However, the methods that Diaz used to remain in power for three and a half decades often went against the grain of human rights and democracy. Any kind of political and cultural opposition was put down ruthlessly during his regime. Also he thought nothing of modifying laws and elections so as to extend his rule. Different sections of the society were played against one another so that the reins of power would always be firmly in Diaz's own hands. But worst of all, the economic reforms he introduced were never intended to benefit the country as a whole. The rural and urban poor, the foot soldiers in the military and the native

Indians not only continued to suffer as they had done for years before, but were dispossessed of communal land holdings as well. On the other hand, the rich and favoured sections of society continued to prosper and were rewarded with powerful appointments by Diaz for their support. No wonder then that the oppressed poor rose against excesses and corruption of the regime in the form of the Mexican Revolution, which in turn threw the country into another decade of conflict and bloodshed.

Today, Porfirio Diaz is remembered in his own country with much more leniency than he was in the last century. The younger generation of Mexicans, especially from the middle class, associates the leader with a time of stability and prosperity. Even then, the legacy of political repression and economic disparity that Diaz left behind served to shape the future of the country in instrumental ways.

□

Vladimir Lenin

D.O.B. – 22nd April, 1870 Country – Russia
D.O.D. – 21st Jan., 1924

Vladimir Lenin was a communist thinker and a leader who led the Russian Revolution of 1917. This revolution deposed the monarchy and established a socialist rule in one of the largest countries of the world. So highly influential were his political views that his ideology – a combination of Marxism and communism – later came to be known as Leninism and inspired countless socialist movements across the globe.

Early Years

Born as Vladimir Ilich Ulyanov on April 22, 1870 in Simbirsk, Russia, Lenin came from a well-educated middle class background. His father was a teacher, who eventually rose to be an inspector of schools. Besides being a government bureaucrat, his father also belonged to the lower end of the hereditary nobility and had a Mongol heritage. Lenin's mother on the other hand had Jewish antecedents. Lenin was the third of six children. One of his siblings did not survive to adulthood but the rest four turned out to be involved – in some capacity or other – in revolutionary activities like him.

While growing up, Lenin was close to his parents and siblings. He was an ardent reader and early on showed a gift for classical languages. In fact, Lenin went on to finish first in his high school class, and did particularly well in Latin and Greek.

Two incidents from Lenin's growing years would come to shape his future life and politics. One of these was the pressure on his father to retire early from an increasingly insecure Tsarist government which suspected public education of spreading revolutionary ideas. Although Lenin's father died in 1866 before the government could take away his job. The effects of threat remained ingrained in young Lenin's mind and nurtured a reaction against the Tsarist rule.

What, however clearly set Lenin on the path of revolution against the monarchy was the arrest and execution of his eldest brother Alexander in 1887 after the latter was found working with a revolutionary group that was planning the assassination of Tsar Alexander III. Since his father had already died, the execution of Alexander left Lenin as the oldest male in the family and with a great deal of responsibility.

Involvement in Politics

In 1887, Lenin enrolled at the Kazan University with the intention of getting a law degree. However, the very first year, he was suspended on account of having participated in an anti-government student demonstration. Lenin thus left for his grandfather's estate in the village of Kokushkino, where his sister Anna was already staying in a form of exile as punishment for her involvement in suspected revolutionary activities.

In the countryside, Lenin busied himself with books and treatises on revolutionary ideologies. Among these one of the most influential book turned out to be novel titled, *What Is To Be Done?* written by Nikolai Chernyshevsky, this revolves around a character named Rakhmetov, who lives and breathes revolutionary politics. However, the book that went on to shape his political philosophy in the most definite manner was *Das Kapital* by Karl Marx which was a heavy indictment of the capitalist society and instead proposes a model of class-less economy, where all are equal. At the same time, Lenin also read up thinkers like Bakunin who were actually opposed to Marx. In the end, Lenin's political beliefs showed the impact of both, his own Russian revolutionary tradition and Marx, whose ideas he went on to modify to some extent.

In 1888, Lenin was allowed to return to Kazan, but still could not go back to the university. Only after his family moved back to Samara, was Lenin given permission to return to his university classes. And yet, he stunned everyone after passing the law university exams with a first class degree and this too, without having attended any lectures or collaborated with anyone over studies.

After obtaining police permission to practice law, Lenin moved to Samara. Here, he began to represent poor Russian peasants in legal battles and over the time, obtained a first-hand view of the oppression of the class system. Feeling the need to pursue a more active political life, Lenin left Samara in the mid-1890s and headed for St. Petersburg, which was the capital city of Russia at the time. It was not long before Lenin began getting in touch with other Marxists here and began organizing other kinds of revolutionary activities. His political actions soon came into sight of the authorities and in December 1895 Lenin along with other Marxists were arrested and imprisoned for fifteen months. But such was the insecurity of the Tsarist government that it decided to send these political activists far from the heart of the country. Consequently, Lenin and a few of his political colleagues, including his fiancée Nadezhda Krupskaya, were exiled to Siberia for no less than three years.

In Siberia, Lenin married Nadezhda and the couple set up a modest home with basic comforts. Life was simple and satisfying for the couple – in their spare time, they studied works of revolutionary thinkers from all over the world and wandered through the village to experience its air of freedom after the restrictions of city life.

After the end of his exile though, Lenin felt the urge to travel to Europe and learn from revolutionary leaders there. He made his way to Munich and there founded a newspaper titled *Iskra* with the aim of fostering a greater understanding between the Russian and European traditions of Marxism.

However growing political unrest in his Russia drew Lenin back and in 1903, at the Second Congress of the Russian Social Democratic Labour Party, he made a vehement case for a more streamlined and disciplined party leadership, one that would be able to better organize, enlist and enthuse the grassroot party workers. "Give us an organization of revolutionaries," Lenin said, "and we will overturn Russia!" His radical stance put him at odds with another leader Julius Martov, whose group of supporters were known as Mensheviks. After Martov staged a walkout with his supporters, Lenin's group, won a slim majority and began to call itself the Bolsheviks.

Political Situation in Russia

In the meantime, Russia got embroiled in the Russo-Japanese War of 1904. Suffering from successive defeats at the hands of the Japanese, Russia found itself overwhelmed both at the diplomatic and economic fronts. Popular discontent against an inept government and the financial hardships suffered by people began to swell across the country. The situation took a turn for the worse when in 1905, a group of unarmed workers in St. Petersburg were fired upon by security forces as they arrived at the city palace to submit a petition to Emperor Nicholas II. By the end of the day, hundreds of workers were dead and many more were wounded in the firing. This event provided the spark for the fire of 1917 Revolution, which would eventually abolish monarchy in Russia.

Realizing the extent of people's discontent, the reigning Tsar of Russia, Nicholas II, initiated some reforms in the political system – the most significant of which the creation of the Duma which would be Russia's first elected legislative assembly.

Despite these political concessions, Lenin was in no mood to relent. Instead, he was eager to push for a full-fledged revolution in Russia which would abolish the monarchy and place power in the hands of the people. But Lenin's propagation of this radical movement brought him in conflict with Martov again. While the latter was in favour of the rise of the bourgeoisie, Lenin was vehement in his support to the proletariat. He believed that it was now time for Russia to transform into a completely socialist state led by the workers of the country. The conflict between the two revolutionary leaders continued till 1912, when the Russian Social-Democratic Workers' Party (RSDWP) split into two factions after Lenin organized his own Bolshevik Congress.

Meanwhile the clouds of the First World War had been gathering on Europe. Lenin saw this as the right opportunity to start a revolution against the government in which the capitalists would be replaced by the proletariat. He declared that the World War was an imperialist war waged by rich capitalists which could never benefit the workers, no matter which side won in the end. But Lenin's call for a pan-European revolution against capitalist system had no many takers as people supported their own governments in the war. Disillusioned but not willing to modify his views, Lenin passed the duration of the war in neutral Switzerland. During this time, he wrote and published one of his most important books, *Imperialism, The Highest Stage of Capitalism* (1916) in which he laid the case that international capitalism was bound to lead to wars of the worst magnitude and intensity.

In 1917, Russia started experiencing the first tremors of the revolution that would go on to change its destiny.

The Tsar was deposed and in place of the monarchy, a provisional government was put in charge. At this time, Lenin was still in exile. Germany agreed to give a passage to Lenin to Russia on the assumption that he would undermine his own country's war efforts against Germany. As expected upon his arrival in Russia, Lenin denounced the provisional government which he claimed were made up of bourgeoisie leaders and exhorted the Bolsheviks to fight for the creation of a Soviet government, one that would be place workers, peasants and soldiers in power.

Rise to Power

Lenin rallied his supporters for most of 1917 till in October, he felt that he had acquired a large enough army of Bolsheviks. Buoyed by their strength, he initiated a coup détat against the provisional government. This came to be known as the 'October Revolution' and ended with Lenin seizing control of the government.

Immediately after the October Revolution, Lenin started taking steps for Russia's exit from the First World War. But most of all he was interested in consolidating his own position as the *de facto* ruler of what was now known as the Union of Socialist Soviet Republic or USSR. He abolished many of the older institutions of the government and put in place new ruling instruments which answered directly to him.

However not everyone was happy with an upheaval of this scale in the country and soon Lenin found himself in conflict with other revolutionary leaders. This led to the onset of a civil war in Russia which raged for three years from 1918 to 1920. On one side were the Red forces led by Lenin and the made up of the Soviet government while on the other side were the White forces, comprised many of former Tsarist generals, admirals and other monarchist supporters. The latter received support in the form of troops and arms from Allied Powers of First World War who were reluctant to see a communist regime set up in Russia. Things came to a head when in 1918, Lenin became the target of an assassination attempt and was shot thrice. Though he survived the attack, his health would never be the same again.

A far more important consequence of the assassination attempt was the hardening of Lenin's stand against his political opponents. Soon Lenin unleashed the full force of government security apparatus on supporters of the Whites – hundreds of people were arrested, shot and executed in a planned repression known as the Red Terror. He ordered the creation of a secret police force to be known as the Cheka. This dreaded force was used to identify and overnight destroy his political rivals. Then there were show trials and concentration camps which led thousands to their deaths. Lenin also ordered the complete elimination of a class called the Kulaks. Finally, any form of religion and public worship was outlawed and in one infamous instance, he exhorted his followers to kill as many members of the church as possible.

In order to bring the country under some semblance of control, Lenin realized that mere ideology won't do. More pressing concerns of the people – like food, livelihood and economic well-being – would have to be addressed. Famine and poverty were rife in society. And in 1921, Lenin found himself confronted by very type of peasant revolts that he had used to bring in the revolution. People fed up of financial hardships were now threatening strikes in cities as well as in the countryside, all of which posed a threat to the stability of Lenin's government. Thus with the end of the civil war, he veered away from his favoured "War Communism" programme and instead launched the New Economic Policy. According to this, farmers were allowed to sell their grain in the open market. In this way, a limited kind of free economic policy was allowed under the New Economic Policy which Lenin felt was necessary to prevent a total economic collapse of the country.

Last Years

Overwrought by years of mental and physical strain, Lenin suffered a series of strokes between 1922 and 1924. These left him partially paralyzed and unable to speak. In fact so depressed was Lenin by his own state of health that many times he tried – unsuccessfully each time – to commit suicide by consuming poison.

Around this time, a new leader was emerging as the dominant leader in USSR - Joseph Stalin who was the general secretary of the Communist Party. In order to safeguard his power, Stalin tried hard to restrict public access to Lenin who was still highly respected by the government and the people of USSR. After Lenin's second stroke, Stalin even tried to prevent Lenin from any source of information on what was happening in the country.

Even then, in his last years, Lenin managed to put together a treatise of sorts in which he criticized the authoritarian character that the present government was taking on. Known as The Testament, it had some harsh words for Stalin especially as Lenin saw how the former had begun to amass great power on the way to becoming a dictator. The Testament also reveals Lenin's awareness of the fact that perhaps the revolution took place a little early in Russia and probably the country was not prepared for the kinds of upheavals that took place then.

On March 10, 1923, Lenin suffered a third and this time far more severe stroke which took away his ability to speak and even forced the curtains to fall on his political work. Nearly ten months later, on January 21, 1924 Lenin passed away in the village, now known as Gorki Leninskiye.

Lenin's Legacy

In an indication of the high stature enjoyed by Lenin during his lifetime and after it, the country decided to embalm his corpse and place it in a mausoleum on Moscow's Red Square for all to see. Because of his revolutionary politics,

Lenin turned out to be not only one of the most important leaders in the history of Russia but also of the world. It was his ideological and political movement that encouraged the people to rise against the Tsarist monarchy and establish a rule of the people. His works have since become the inspiration for revolutions and movements across the world, despite sometimes making for a contradictory and initially naïve programme.

□

Adolph Hitler

D.O.B. – 20th April, 1889 Country –Austria
D.O.D. – 30th April, 1945

If there is one name in history that has become synonymous with the worst excesses of dictatorship, it is that of Adolph Hitler. The Fuhrer or Leader as liked to be known not only ordered one of largest massacres in history but with his expansionist policies, changed the map of the globe. Hitler was instrumental in precipitating the Second World War which in turn altered the territorial limits of countries and entire continents.

Early Life

Born on 20 April 1889 in the small Austrian town of Braunau, Hitler came from a modest background. His mother Klara, came from a poor peasant family while his father Alois went on to become a senior official in the customs department. When Hitler was 3 years old, the family moved from Austria to Germany. An important childhood event which left a mark on the young Hitler's emotional being was the death of his younger brother Edmund in 1900 after which he became aloof and an introvert.

Hitler did not do particularly well in school. Though in primary school, he was popular among his classmates, as he grew up, he preferred the company of younger boys before whom he would act out scenes from the Boer War. Hitler could not keep up with studies and after failing his exams at the age of fifteen, he dropped out from school.

Hitler's father died suddenly in 1903. With the money left to him upon his father's death, Hitler set off for Vienna where he intended to study Arts – the only subject that perhaps he loved at school. However, his applications to both the School of Architecture and the Vienna Academy of Art were rejected, the latter not once, but twice. In the meantime, Hitler found work as a casual labourer and even dabbled in painting. However, money quickly ran out and he was forced to find refuge in a homeless shelter, where he remained for several years.

Political Involvement

It was during these days of struggle in Vienna that Hitler first became interested in politics. Those were the days of Austro-Hungarian supremacy in Germany and Hitler chafed at the foreign influence in his homeland. Also he later looked upon this time of hardship as the source of his anti-Semitism, though there is some disagreement among historians on that.

The outbreak of the First World War in 1914 gave Hitler an opportunity to express his fervent nationalism. He promptly enlisted, though officially he was still an Austrian citizen. Hitler was sent to the frontlines where he saw action in a number of important battles, even being wounded at Some. After the war, Hitler was honoured for bravery, and decorated with the Iron Cross First Class as well as the Black Wound Badge.

However, the outcome of the First World War left Hitler embittered. He was appalled at the terms of the Treaty of Versailles which Germans felt was loaded against their country. Several harsh political and economic penalties were set against Germany in the treaty which led to a wave of dissatisfaction among Germans and stoked the fire of nationalism.

Hitler continued to work for the army even after the end of World War I. As a part of his duties as an intelligence officer, was ordered to monitor the activities of the DAP or the German Workers' Party. This was a political group founded by Anton Drexler that was based on strong nationalist, anti-Semitic and anti-Marxist tenets. Hitler became impressed by the ideological tenets of the party and in 1919 he became an official member of DAP.

Hitler's entry into DAP saw the party going through a visible transformation. Not only was the name changed to *Nationalsozialistische Deutsche Arbeiterpartei* or National Socialist German Workers' Party (Nazi), but Hitler himself designed the party flag which displayed a black swastika in a white circle against a red background. The tone of the party speeches too changed under Hitler which took on a more combative tone and were fiercely directed against political opponents, the Treaty of Versailles as well as Marxists and Jews. Not surprisingly, when Drexler stepped down from the party leadership in 1921, Hitler became the new NSDAP chairman.

Soon Hitler's party and his violent speeches began attracting other aggressive elements of German political scene. One such supporter was army captain Ernst Rohm, who headed the Nazi paramilitary organization, the Sturmabteilung (SA). Around this time, Germany was in the grip of terrible economic conditions and the common people reeling under hardship found in Hitler's speeches an echo of their conditions. Consequently, support for the Nazi grew and by 1923, its membership had crossed 56,000 members with many more supporters. As Hitler's popularity increased, the SA was regularly tasked with safeguarding meetings and even using violence against rival politicians.

On November 8, 1923, Hitler ordered an attack on a public meeting in Munich. Known as the Beer Hall Putsch, the SA stormed a large beer hall where around 3000 people were present. With Hitler announcing that the national revolution had begun and a new government was being set up, the SA tried to seize the building. The ensuing violence resulted in twenty deaths and capture of Hitler three days later along with many of his supporters.

Tried and convicted for high treason, Hitler was sentenced to one year in prison. It was during this time that he dictated to his deputy Rudolf Hess, his autobiography *Mein Kamp "My Struggle"*, which was also an exposition of his political philosophy. For the first time, he clearly talked about his plans for a German state based upon the supremacy of race as well as that of expanding German influence and territory in Europe.

Rise to Power

Hitler's massive political appeal became official when in the presidential elections of 1932, his party came second, seizing more than 35 percent of the vote in the final election. In fact, such was his popularity that President Hindenburg much against his wishes was forced to appoint Hitler as a Chancellor.

The official appointment was the start of his *de facto* dictatorship since now Hitler had the opportunity to bring in sweeping changes to the government. After a suspect fire at the Reichstag, Hitler brought into force the Reichstag Fire Decree which suspended the basic rights of citizens and allowed the law to detain anyone without trial. Another significant measure was the passing of the Enabling Act, according to which, Hitler's cabinet was granted full legislative powers for a period of four years and was allowed to bypass the stipulations under the German Constitution.

Now that Hitler had solidified his grip on the executive and legislative arms of the government. He turned his attention towards decimating all political opposition. Most of the rival political parties were threatened into disbanding and those who didn't agree were exterminated. Eventually on July 14, 1933, the Nazi Party was declared the only legal political party in Germany.

Hitler knew that his position would remain weak unless he gets the entire military under his control. Consequently, he ordered a purge in the military services which continued from June 30 to July 2, 1934. In the incident which came to be known as the Night of the Long Knives, SA leaders like Ernst Rohm, along with many other political rivals of Hitler, were rounded up and executed.

In August 1934, only a day before the death of President Hindenburg, the cabinet passed a law which abolished the office of President and combining its powers with those of the Chancellor. This made Hitler not only the head of the government but also the head of the state and as such also the supreme commander of the armed forces. In this way, Hitler's control over Germany was now complete.

Road to Second World War

Now that he was in full control of national politics, Hitler turned his attention to the world scene. For long, the Germans had been chafing under what they considered extremely unfair terms of the Treaty of Versailles and which was primarily blamed for Germany's economic hardships. Hitler was now determined to make right the wrong and he compelled European leaders to sign the Munich Agreement. This reversed some of the injunctions of the Treaty of Versailles and accordingly returned the Sudetenland districts to Germany. This diplomatic win added to Hitler's reputation and he was not only hailed by his own people but also nominated *Time* magazine's Man of the Year for 1938.

But Hitler was not to be appeased with mere modifications of any treaty and instead had his sights set on more substantial territorial gains. On 1 September 1939, Germany invaded Poland which resulted with Britain and France declaring war on Germany. Thus began the Second World War.

Instead of being concerned at Britain and France joining forces against him, Hitler pushed even further ahead. In 1940, he invaded Scandinavia as well as France, Luxembourg, the Netherlands and Belgium. He planned to cow down Britain with a sleet of bombing raids over the island nation. And in order to bulk up his offensive, Hitler also brought Japan and Italy to his side, thus forming the group of Axis Powers.

Hitler's bravura increased with each country succumbing to his advancing forces. On June 22, 1944 however he sent a three million-strong German army into the Soviet Union, thus shattering a non-aggression pact that had been signed with Joseph Stalin. Though the German forces could not reach Moscow and had to retreat in December 1941, they managed to capture a sizeable Russian territory. A far more important consequence of the German invasion was that it pitched Russia into the Second World War, a formidable enemy that would eventually contribute to Hitler's downfall.

However, the event which would really go on to turn the tide of the Second World War was Japan's attack on Pearl Harbour, an American naval station in Hawaii. This cemented United States' involvement in the World War and now the other half of the world came together against Hitler and his supporters. The Allies consisted of the world's financial superpower United States, the country with the largest army, Russia as well as the largest empire, Britain.

Beginning of the End

Against such overwhelming opposition, Hitler's military offensive began to suffer and one expensive defeat followed another. In late 1942, the Germans lost the war to capture the Suez Canal, a channel that was of great strategic importance. Next the German army suffered crucial setbacks at the Battle of Stalingrad and the Battle of Kursk. Finally on June 6, 1944, after a great deal of preparation, came the

D-Day when arn ies from western Allied countries, landed on the shores of northern France.

From then on it was only a matter of time before Germany was brought down on its knees. For a long time though Hitler continued in a state of denial during which his forces made many high-priced mistakes. In 1944, he was the target of an assassination attempt which though unsuccessful heightened his sense of terror and paranoia and he responded by further distancing himself from the situation on the ground. Finally in 1945, realization dawned on Hitler that Germany would soon buckle under. The Soviet forces had pushed the German army back into Western Europe while the Allied armies were already making their way into German territory.

With defeat staring at Hitler, ultimately he married Eva Braun, his girlfriend (having long time affair with her), on April 29, 1945, in a small civil ceremony in his Berlin bunker. The next day, he received the news of the assassination of Benito Mussolini, the Italian dictator and his partner from the Axis Group. Afraid that a same fate would await him too, Hitler decided to commit suicide with his wife on April 30, 1945, the very next day after their wedding. Instead of being buried, their bodies burned in the bombed-out garden behind the Reich Chancellery. Finally on May 2, 1945 Berlin fell to the Allied Forces, thus bringing down the curtains on the most widespread and gruesome war in history.

Social Measures

The reign of the Nazi party began with certain social reforms in 1932. Hitler ordered anti-smoking campaigns throughout the country and encouraged his followers to give up alcohol and meat. Soon, however, these measures took on aspects of racism. Racial hygiene and racial pollution became the driving philosophy for his social and political injunctions. Accordingly, laws were passed which forbade marriages between Jews and non-Jews and which denied the benefits of citizenship to non-Aryans.

The Holocaust

The worst of his anti-Semitism took shape in the Holocaust which continued from 1939 to 1945. As the Second World War raged across the Europe, the Nazis ordered the extermination of about six million Jews, which made up a staggering two-thirds of the Jewish population in Europe. Jews from across territories under German control were brought into concentration camps and then murdered by gunshots, in gas chambers or by other means. Overall the Holocaust and its related violence led to the deaths of 11 million to 14 million people – one of the largest mass murders in the history of the world. Incidentally, Hitler never associated himself directly with the Holocaust. There are no records of him personally visiting the concentration camps and nor did he speak publicly about the killings.

While the Holocaust is remembered as the most brutal aspect of Hitler's eugenics policies, there were many other groups that were targeted with violence. Both children and adults with physical and developmental disabilities were considered a blot on the Aryan race under Nazi philosophy and in order to maintain the supposed supremacy of the Aryan race, Hitler authorized a euthanasia program for disabled adults. Likewise communists and trade union workers were rounded up and executed for political opposition. Again Poles, Jehovah's witnesses and homosexuals were exterminated for no other reason than that they espoused to different cultural, national or sexual choices.

Hitler's Legacy

Among the dictators of the world, there is probably no other figure who has changed the course of history in such a decisive manner. Hitler's policies of German expansionism and militarization set in motion the Second World War which turned out to have lasting consequences for the economic and political geography of Europe. Since the mid-twentieth century, the world came to be divided into the American-led Western bloc and the Soviet bloc consisting of its mainly socialist supporters. This eventually led to the Cold War in the second half of the twentieth century – a state of conflict where the threat of nuclear war loomed large till in relations between United States and USSR thawed in the 1990s. The economic consequences of Hitler's policies were even harsher – the central and eastern parts of Europe were unable to bear the brunt of the Second World War and got sucked in the morass of financial hardship and Soviet control.

Germany, on whose prestige and supremacy, Hitler rode his political ambitions, was itself divided into two parts – the Capitalist, West Germany with its capital in Berlin and the Communist East Germany with Bonn as its capital. The Berlin Wall dividing West and East Germany became a symbol of this artificial, cruel barrier put in place by governments with complete disregard for the wishes of the ordinary German people. This continued to the state of affairs till popular sentiment prevailed in and the Berlin Wall was demolished leading to the reunification of Germany.

However by far, most striking are the human costs of Hitler's reign of terror. Never before had the policies of any single leader led to this scale of human suffering. Whether directly or indirectly, Hitler and his party were responsible for the death of an estimated 40 million people, including about 27 million in the Soviet Union alone. Not surprisingly the world remembers Adolf Hitler as one of the most powerful and brutal dictators in the history of the world.

☐

Ho Chi Minh

D.O.B. – 19th May, 1890
D.O.D. – 2nd Sept., 1969

Country – Vietnam

Ho Chi Minh was a Vietnamese statesman and leader who fought against French colonialisms and founded the Democratic State of Vietnam in North Vietnam. Popularly known as 'Uncle Ho', he exercised absolute power in the country for more than twenty-five years. Today even after of his death, Ho Chi Minh is regarded as the symbol of Vietnamese struggle from colonial rule as well as the political leader, who inflicted a long costly war against anti-communist South Vietnam and its powerful ally, the United States.

Early Life

Born as Nguyen Sinh Cung on May 19, 1890, the Vietnamese leader adopted the name Ho Chi Minh later which means "the Bringer of Light". He came from a small Central Vietnamese village, Hoang Tru, which was then part of French Indo-China. For the most of part of his childhood, Ho was brought up by his mother, Loan, along with his two other siblings. During this time, his father Nguyen Sinh Sac was preparing for the Confucian civil service exams so as to get an appointment as a local government official. Despite having a hard life working on the family's small paddy field, Ho's mother would regale the children with stories of ancient Vietnamese literature and folk heroes. This probably planted the earliest seeds of national pride in young Ho's mind, which eventually went on to take shape of the political ideology of nationalism.

For a time, Nguyen Sinh Sac worked as a tutor at the village school and during this time young Ho quickly picked up lessons meant for the older children. By the time Ho was old enough to attend school, the family had moved to Hue. Here the boy learnt the Chinese language and became familiar with the classics of Confucian literature and philosophy. When young Ho was ten years old, his father gave him another name, Nguyen Tat Than, meaning 'Nguyen the Accomplished'.

In 1901, Ho's mother died in childbirth while the infant survived for only another year. After this, Ho was sent to a French school in Hue to acquire a professional degree and consequently he graduated to become a teacher.

Despite having a stable job, Ho was not satisfied with life and decided to take up employment of a kind that will help him to see the world. With this aim in mind, in 1911 Ho became a cook's helper aboard a ship that was travelling from Asia to Africa and Europe. Though historians are not certain the exact route that Ho took on his sea voyages, he apparently stopped at ports along the coasts of Asia, Africa and France in Europe. Ho was particularly interested in the behaviour of French people since Vietnam was a French colony. Along his travels, he began to feel that the fault lay not in any particular race or nationality but the very system of colonialism resulted in exploitation and oppression.

Ho's sea travels also took him to United States where he stayed for a few years, once in New York City and another time in Boston, where he apparently worked as a baker's assistant. Observing life in America, he realized the value of independence. Here he saw Asians making a better life for themselves as compared to those living in their own countries but under colonial rule. During his time in America, Ho was also impressed by the theory of self-determination as outlined by President Woodrow Wilson, according to which people should be allowed to determine their own political system. Ironically though, Wilson was a covert racist, who believed that only the 'white' people of Europe were deserving of self-determination and even in his own country, brought back the practice of segregation in White House.

Involvement with Communist Party

1918 saw the conclusion of the First World War whereupon the heads of major European countries came together to work out an armistice. This resulted in 1919 Paris Peace Conference where for the first time many Asian and African countries raised their voices for the right to self-determination. Among the proponents of such demands, was Ho, who now adopted the name of Nguyen Ai Quoc - "Nguyen who loves his country." Again and again, he tried to present a petition to the French representatives and their allies, demanding independence for Indo-China but could not be heard in any significant quarter.

While the ruling class of Europe remained unsympathetic to the demands of self-determination by Asians and Africans, the communists of France proved to be more sympathetic. Karl Marx had already described Imperialism as the last stage of capitalism. Taking this point of view, the French Communist Party seemed more amenable to the concerns of those living under colonial systems. Thus, Ho decided to read more about Marxism and communism and eventually decided to ally himself with these political parties.

After picking up the fundamentals of communist ideology from France, Ho began to look for opportunities where he could actively pursue his political commitment. Thus, he decided to head for the Soviet Union in 1923 and began to work for the Comintern or the Third Communist

International. In Moscow, Ho became acquainted with the ways of planning and carrying out insurrections and also learnt how to get the upper hand over government forces with their larger armies and resources. Ho was however interested more in the practicalities of organizing revolutions rather than in competing theories of communism, which in fact was leading to the growing conflict between Trotsky and Stalin at that time.

Though Ho had picked up valuable lessons about revolutionary activities in USSR, he realized that if he was to launch a successful revolution in his home country, he needed to set up a rebel base closer to Vietnam. With his aim, he travelled to China and in November 1924; he arrived at Canton or present-day Guangzhou. At the time, China was in a state of political flux following the dissolution of the Quing dynasty in 1911 as well as the death of self-proclaimed Great Emperor of China, General Yuan Shi-Kai in 1916. Different leaders had sprung up in different parts of the country – while the Chinese hinterland was in the grip of local warlords, the cities of the eastern coast were home to the growing Chinese Communist Party, led by Sun Yat Sen. General Chiang Kai-Shek was another important leader in China who like Sun Yat Sen was in favour of growth of the nationalism but on the other hand, who was completely opposed to the spread of communism.

Ho Chi Minh stayed in China for more than two years. He used this time to gather funds and supporters for his armed struggle against French colonial government in Indo-China. He not only managed to train around hundred Indo-Chinese operatives but also taught the basic principles of communism to local Chinese people and on one occasion, even helped to organize the peasants of Guangdong Province to strive for their cause.

However in April 1927, Chiang Kai Shek and his Kuomintang Party began a brutal purge of communists in China. In the bloodshed that followed around 12000 communist workers, supporters and even civilians with no party leaning were massacred. The purge would go on to become infamous in Chinese history for claiming at least 300,000 lives across the nation over the following year. To escape the witch-hunt, while the Chinese Communist Party members escaped into the forests and mountains, Ho Chi Minh and other Cominterns realized that they would need to leave China if they wanted to save their lives.

Rise to Power

By this time, Ho's reputation as an ardent Communist Party worker had reached the ears of the French colonial government in China and it was not willing to allow him entry into Indo-China. As a result, he decided to head for the British colony of Hong Kong under a forged visa with the name of Ly Thuy. However before long, he was found out and ordered to leave the colony within twenty-four hours.

Once again, Ho made his way to USSR, this time to the Pacific Coast city of Vladivostok. From there he embarked the Trans Siberian Railway with the aim of reaching Moscow. His agenda at the Soviet capital was clear – to appeal to the top honchos of Comintern to lend him the funds and resources so as to be able to launch an armed struggle against the French colonial government in Indo-China. For this purpose, Ho planned to make neighbouring country of Siam, now known as Thailand, his headquarters.

Though Ho Chi Minh did visit Thailand in July 1928, he was not yet able to set up his base for the planned armed struggle in his home country. Instead he continued with his travels through many countries of Asia and Europe; for the following thirteen years he passed in and out of Italy, India, China, Soviet Union and British Hong Kong in an attempt to rally support for his cause – gathering men, arms and money.

The onset of the Second World War and France's defeat to Germany finally gave Ho Chi Minh the opportunity that he was looking for. In 1941, he returned to his home country with his closest supporters, Vo Nguyen Giap and Pham Van Dong. Once back in Vietnam, Ho founded the Viet Minh, or League for the Independence of Vietnam. However in the process, he had to spend eighteen months in a Chinese prison as he had sought help from Chinese communists for which he was arrested and convicted by Chiang Kai-Shek's anti-Communist government.

The Allied victory in 1945 saw the exit of Japanese forces from Vietnam. Though Vietnam was officially independent, the erstwhile French colonial government had placed French-educated Emperor Bai Dao as a puppet monarch with the aim of continuing to influence Vietnam's policies.

Ho Chi Minh ordered the Viet Minh forces to take as much control of the country as possible and led by Vo Nguyen Giap. They were able to capture the northern city of Hanoi. This led to the established of the Democratic State of Vietnam, more commonly as North Vietnam, and Ho Chi Minh became its president. Bai Dao realized it would be prudent to abdicate but by this time, a division of the country was inevitable. The southern part of the country came to be known as South Vietnam which along with its capital, Saigon was controlled by French military troops.

In the meantime, Chiang Kai Shek's forces started bearing upon the border of North Vietnam in keeping with the Chinese leader's agreement with Allied Forces. Ho overcame his long-term colonial hatred and reached out to the French authorities with the main aim of rooting out Kai-Shek's forces but also to push for a French recognition of Vietnam's independence and an eventual re-unification of North and South Vietnam.

The First Vietnam War

In October 1946, however things came to a head, when following a clash between French authorities and Vietnamese people over custom duties in the port city of

Haiphong, a French fleet opened fire and left more than six thousand Vietnamese civilians dead. Though Ho tried his best to find a peaceful resolution, his more militant followers wanted revenge for the French action and war broke out in December 1946.

For the next eight years, the Viet Minh was locked in battle with French colonial forces. Since the latter had the advantages of more advanced equipment and wider resources, Ho Chi Minh decided to use guerilla tactics against the French army based on hit-and-run tactics as well as their superior knowledge of the terrain. At the same time the Viet Minh received some support from Soviet Union as well as China, where Chiang Kai Shek had been defeated by the ardent communist Mao Zedong.

The decisive event of the First Vietnam War was the Battle of Dien Bien Phu, in which the French forces finally catapulted to the guerilla warfare of Viet Minh and agreed to pull out completely from Vietnam. This battle eventually went down in history as the inspiration for Algerian struggle against French colonial might.

However, the human costs – on both sides – turned out to be immense. By the end of the First Vietnam War, the Viet Minh had lost 500,000 of its people while the casualties on the French side touched 90,000. Among the Vietnamese civilians, a staggering 200000 and 300000 people lay dead. According to the terms of the Geneva Convention, Ho Chi Minh was appointed the *de facto* president of northern Vietnam and in South Vietnam, a pro-US capitalist leader, Ngo Dinh Diem, assume. Most importantly, the convention mandated that elections should be held across Vietnam in 1956.

The Second Vietnam War

The United States however was not willing to accede to the terms marking the end of the First Vietnam War. According to the reigning "domino effect" theory of the time, the US feared that the fall of one country to communist forces – like what had happened in China – would influence other states in the region to follow suit and eventually communism would emerge the dominant political system in South East Asia. This compelled America to put its weight behind Ngo Dinh Diem, as he announced the cancellation of 1956 elections, which would have most likely unified Vietnam.

The cancellation of elections prompted Ho Chi Minh to call for action against the pro-America South Vietnam government. The Viet Minh forces began to wage guerilla war in South Vietnam which in turn prompted the US to expand its involvement till North and South Vietnam were locked in full-fledged war, supported by their respective allies.

In order to devote more time and energy to rallying support for North Vietnam from international communist powers, Ho Chi Minh appointed Le Duan as the political leader of the country. However, Ho retained all effective authority and continued to be the power behind the titular president.

As the Second Vietnam War dragged on, Ho realized the toll that was taking on his army, countrymen and the allies. He then planned the Tet Offensive as a way of breaking the stalemate and forcing the conflict to conclusion. Strategically, the Tet Offensive was a disaster, both for Ho's forces and its allies, the Viet Cong. However, the initiative had the unforeseen advantage of focusing international limelight on the situation in Vietnam. The international outcry against US involvement in the war began to get louder until domestic public opinion in the US squarely supported American pull-out from the region. Ho Chi Minh realized that it was only a matter of time that US was forced to withdraw and that till that time all he had to do was to wait it out.

Though Ho's calculations would prove to be correct, he would not live to see the withdrawal of American troops from Vietnam. On September 2, 1969, the 79-year-old leader of North Vietnam suffered a heart failure and died in Hanoi.

Legacy

Such was the popularity of Brother Ho that when in April 1975 North Vietnamese troops entered the city of Saigon following American withdrawal, they carried posters of their dear leader in remembrance and respect. Not long after Saigon, the erstwhile capital of South Vietnam, would be officially renamed Ho Chi Minh City in 1976.

Ho Chi Minh is chiefly remembered today as the leader who led a long, arduous but ultimately successful struggle for Vietnamese independence against French colonial forces. However, his legacy is not without its share of controversy. Though he endures as the symbol of Vietnamese independence, the ruling Communist Party in the country that lays sole claim to the heritage of Vietnamese stalwart, is today accused of corruption, greed and misrule. What should be recognized is that at the end of the day the legacy of a leader of a stature like Ho Chi Minh cannot be restricted within narrow political lines and belongs to every son and daughter of Vietnam.

□

Joseph Stalin

D.O.B. – 18th Dec., 1878 | Country – Russia
D.O.D. – 5th March, 1953

A towering figure in the history of USSR, Joseph Stalin was the supreme leader of the country from 1878 to 1953. He is credited with transforming USSR from an agricultural country to an industrial and military giant. Indeed, it is largely on the strength of these fundamentals that USSR continued to be the only superpower other than the US for much of the twentieth century. However, Stalin was also a feared dictator and his policies were often brutally enforced, whether or not they were meant for the benefit of the country.

Early Life

Stalin was born as Josef Vissarionovich Djugashvili in the small town of Gori, Georgia, which was then part of the Russian empire. Like the name he took later – Stalin translates as "man of steel" in the Russian, Stalin also fashioned his own date of birth – December 21, 1879 though historians now believe that he was actually born on December 18, 1878, or if one follows the Old Style Julian calendar, on December 6, 1878.

Stalin belonged to a family of humble background. His father, Besarion Jughashvili, was a cobbler, while his mother Ketevan Geladze, washed clothes for other people. When he was seven, Stalin came down with smallpox, which left scars on his face and a slight deformity on his left arm. Unfortunately, young Stalin was humiliated by the village children for his physical defects and this in turn instilled a cruel streak in him, turning him into a bully.

Being a devout Russian Orthodox Christian, Stalin's mother wanted him to join the priesthood. Thus, in 1888, the young Stalin was enrolled into church school in Gori. He was a good student and after passing out from school had little problems landing a scholarship to Tiflis Theological Seminary in 1894.

Political Activism

In 1895, Stalin came got to know a few people belonging to a secret political organization known as Messame Dassy. One of the demands of this party was Georgia be allowed to cede from the Russian empire and recognized as an independent country. Among the people from Messame Dassy who befriended Stalin were a few socialists who introduced him to the writings of Karl Marx and Vladimir Lenin. Eventually, in 1898, Stalin became a formal member of the group.

Despite doing well in studies, Stalin dropped out of the seminary school in 1899. There are varied accounts of why this happened. According to the official sources, Stalin could not pay the tuition fees and thus had to drop out. Other accounts point out to the ideological conflict between supporting the socialists in their opposition to the Tsarist regime of Nicholas II and studying at the traditional school which was obviously patronized by the Tsar. Anyway, after leaving school, he tried to get a job and finally managed to find work as a tutor and later as a clerk at the Tiflis Observatory. In 1901, he became an official member of the Social Democratic Labor Party and worked full-time for the revolutionary movement. In 1902, he was arrested for planning a labour strike and as punishment was sent to a labour camp in Siberia.

Stalin however could not be exiled for long and he managed to flee from the prisoner's camp in Siberia. After his escape, Stalin had to spend many months in hiding from the Okhranka, the dreaded secret police belonging to the Tsar.

Rise to Power

Though Stalin had superior organizational skills, he lacked the vision as well as the ideals of leaders like Lenin and Trotsky. Instead, he was an expert in the more tedious aspects of the revolution like publishing leaflets, organizing meetings as well as launching strikes and demonstrations. But apart from these, money was the top priority for the revolution. And for this purpose, Stalin went so far as to resort to robbery, extortion and kidnapping. In fact, in 1907 a bank robbery took place in Tiflis, which became notorious for the involvement of Stalin. It was reported that the robbery had ended in deaths of many people and the stealing of 250,000 rubals which was later calculated at $3.4 million in US dollars.

Though the Russian Revolution of 1917 overthrew the Russian monarchy, it also resulted in great confusion. A provisional government had been put in place but this neither carried weight with the opposition members nor could prove popular with the people. As such Vladimir Lenin saw that it was time to take matters in his own hands. He exhorted people to seize land from rich farmers and factories from big industrialists. By October 1917, the Russian Revolution had come to a close and now the Bolsheviks were on their way to form the government.

Despite some attempts to bring about stability by Lenin, the nation's politics in USSR at that time was in a mess. Different political leaders intent on enhancing their own positions and control without caring much about how the nation should be governed. In 1922, a new post – that of the general secretary of the Communist Party was created and Stalin was invited to take charge. This gave Stalin an opportunity to control all the members of party through appointments and he used this to build his fundamental support base.

By the time of Lenin's death in 1924, Stalin had become extremely powerful. Nearly all top-ranking officials of the USSR Communist Party now owed their appointments to Stalin and hence could not afford to oppose him in any way. Any rival politician whose influence could be a threat to Stalin was shunted to remote posts in the country or even sent abroad like to the Americas or to Europe – something which befell as well-respected a leader as Leon Trotsky, who at one time was being considered the successor of Lenin.

Even after surrounding himself with supporters in the Communist Party, Stalin was not satisfied. Such was his hunger for absolute power that he started a series of purges with the aim of completely wiping out any hint of opposition. Night-time raids became a regular affair during which anyone could be whisked away by the secret police, arrested and subject to fake trials. Anyone who had ever dared to speak out against Stalin was now charged of being an ally of capitalist nations, convicted of being "enemies of the people" and finally executed. While the purge had begun with weeding out opposition in the higher party ranks, Stalin's paranoia now knew no bounds and even minor local officials with no link to him were accused of counter-revolutionary activities and punished.

Economic Measures

The Bolshevik Revolution had introduced important agricultural reforms, primary among which was to give plots of land to small farmers. However, Stalin sought to reverse this and during the 1920s and '30s he initiated policies to set up vast agricultural communes on which farmers would work and receive wages. This led to the seizure of lands from the peasants and consequently led to extreme dissent in the peasant class. They resented being reverted back to the position of landless workers which was practically the same as serfs that had existed during the time of Russian monarchy.

However like any dictator, Stalin refused to entertain any resistance to his draconian policies. Any resistance from the farmers to giving up their lands was met with brutal force. Millions of people around this time were imprisoned, executed or exiled to the labour camps of Gulag in snow-bound Siberia. The few who escaped punishment found themselves staring at hunger and starvation brought about by the loss of their farms and livelihood.

Another aspect of Stalin's reformist measures was large-scale industrialization. Large factories and heavy industries were set up in USSR during this time which in the initial period at least increased industrial production. However with passing time, the true cost of the rapid industrialization policy became clearer as large swathes of countryside suffered environmental damage and the close-knit community ties of agricultural villages disappeared along with its traditions.

The Second World War

Stalin's overconfidence in domestic policies had an inevitable impact in his foreign policies too. Despite the misgivings of some leaders in his own government and commanders in his own military, Stalin went ahead and signed a non-aggression pact with Adolph Hitler and Nazi Germany. This treaty was touted as a great victory of foreign policy and Stalin was depicted as an astute statesman, both in domestic and world affairs.

However in the summer of 1941, Stalin was jolted out of his complacency, when Hitler broke the pact and launched a blitzkrieg on the eastern German front. Completely unprepared for an attack of such intensity, the Soviet armies suffered huge losses initially. By the time Stalin was able to get his act together, he found that German armies had not only taken control of Ukraine and Belarus but its artillery was bearing down on Leningrad. What made matters worse was the vacuum in leadership. Stalin had carried out such a vicious purge in the military that there were now hardly enough commanders to lead the ranks by strategic expertise or example of personal courage.

It was now up to the resourcefulness of the Soviet army and the bravery of the ordinary Russians to counter the invading German forces. In 1943, the Germans were forced to retreat from Stalingrad and in 1944, the Soviet army had broken Hitler's eastern front and was also liberating east European countries that had fallen to German aggression. All this was even before D-Day when the Allies would land on the French coast to mount the largest planned offensive against Germany.

Beginning of the Cold War

Though USSR was on the same side as Britain and United States in the Second World War, Stalin had long been suspicious of the Western powers. In a series of meeting with Western leaders between 1943 and 1944, Stalin had managed to convince the Allied Powers to open up a second front against Germany. Again in 1945 at a meeting in Yalta, Crimea both the British Prime Minster Churchill and the US President Roosevelt agreed to give Joseph Stalin a free hand in reorganizing the governments of Eastern Europe that the Soviet army had liberated from German control. In exchange, Stalin agreed to launch an offensive against Japan once Germany was defeated.

However at the Potsdam Conference in 1945, Stalin was met with different set of conditions. The Allied leaders had changed – the United States was now represented by President Trueman while the British Prime Minister was

Clement Attlee. Thus, negotiations took on a more negative turn – while the Western powers were suspicious of Stalin's plans for post-war Japan, Stalin felt he was being sidelined to the margins of the theatre of war.

With the dropping of the atomic bombs on the Japanese cities of Hiroshima and Nagasaki, the Second World War was brought to a decisive end. Japan succumbed to the Allied Powers but Stalin felt cheated out of his opportunity to play a role in the Eastern country's fortunes. Consequently, his suspicions about the Western powers intensified and he became convinced that they were planning a capitalist invasion of USSR. Between 1945 and 1948, Stalin set about putting up Communist governments in many Eastern European countries with the aim of creating an immense "buffer zone" that would protect Mother Russia from decadent Western capitalists. Eventually, this would come to be known as the Soviet bloc and would be pitted against the Western powers during the period of the Cold War. Stalin's actions in creating such a "buffer zone" were interpreted by the Western nations as an attempt to expand communism throughout Europe. In response, they formed the North Atlantic Treaty Organization or NATO as a way of countering Soviet influence.

Like any other dictator, Stalin's megalomania now knew no bounds. Feeling slighted by the Allied Powers, he was determined to gain full control on the German capital city Berlin. With this mind, in 1948, he ordered an economic blockade on the city. The Western nations responded by airlifting supplies into the city and thus demolished Stalin's plans of bring Berlin down to its knees.

Despite having suffered diplomatic setbacks, Stalin refused to see reason and was obsessed at getting back at Western nations. With this intention, he encouraged North Korean Communist leader Kim Il Sung to invade South Korea. But soon United States joined the fray and came out in support of South Korea, both with diplomatic and military resources. In fact, USSR found itself sidelined in the world forum as well. Stalin had ordered the USSR representative to boycott the Security Council as a way of protest when the United Nations had refused to accept the newly formed Communist People's Republic of China into the international organization. When the Security Council took up a vote to pass a resolution in support of South Korea, USSR was unable to use its veto because of Stalin's earlier shortsightedness.

Last Years

From the late 1950s, Stalin began keeping unwell. When a plot to assassinate him was unearthed, Stalin's earlier paranoia returned and he ordered the chief of his secret police to launch a widespread purge to root out all opposition elements. However before the purge could be carried out, Stalin died on March 5, 1953.

His Legacy

Stalin ruled USSR with an iron fist for more than two decades. In that time, he ensured that all power resided with him and effectively wiped out all forms of political opposition. Because he enjoyed absolute power, he was able to overturn the country's economic policy, transforming a largely peasant economy to a modern industrialized nation. Also his stewardship of the country during the Second World War increased his domestic and international clout. Despite being taken off guard by Hitler's treachery, the Soviet army was eventually successful in forcing the feared German army to retreat from Stalingrad. Moreover, the liberation of many East European countries even before the Allied Forces had got its act together, convinced the world that no major decision relating to the Second World War could be taken without Stalin's participation.

Despite paving the way for USSR to emerge as a superpower, Stalin's legacy is shadowed by the extensive abuse of power during his regime. As a dictator, he ensured that there was critique to his policies or the slightest challenge to his authority. Millions of people were arrested, imprisoned, executed or sent to Siberian labour camps on the slightest suspicion of opposition and often without any reason at all. The 'Gulag' or the government agency that administered forced labour during Stalin's time had gone down in history as among the most brutal instruments of political oppression that ever existed in human society.

□

General Franco

D.O.B. – 4th Dec., 1892 Country – Spain
D.O.D. – 20th Nov., 1975

One of the longest reigning dictators in modern Europe, General Francisco Franco ruled Spain from 1939 till his death in 1975. He was the driving force in the Spanish Civil War, which overthrew a tottering Leftist Republic and brought in its place, Franco's military dictatorship. During this time, he took the title of "El Caudillo" or The Leader. Though he introduced some reforms to make Spain economically self-sufficient, his rule was also marked by widespread abuse of power, repression of political opponents as well as the destruction of Basque and Catalan culture. However towards the end of his reign, his dictatorial stronghold relaxed to some extent, and after his death, democracy returned to Spain.

Early Life

Born as Francisco Paulino Hermenegildo Teódulo Franco Bahamonde in El Ferrol, Spain, in 1892, the future Spanish dictator came from a long tradition of military professionals, especially serving in the navy. His father was an officer in the Spanish Naval Administrative Corps and his elder brother was also a naval officer. Till the age of twelve, Franco was educated in a Catholic school, after which he enrolled into a naval secondary school with the intention of later applying to the Naval Academy. However, a shortage of resources prompted the government to stop accepting naval cadets and this compelled Franco to sign up at the Infantry Academy in Toledo instead. After three years, he graduated from the Academy as an infantry officer and was posted to El Ferrol for a brief while.

Military Career

However, Franco was interested to see action and thus in 1912, he volunteered to go to Morocco where the Spanish forces were trying to quell an insurgency. The very next year, Franco was promoted to the rank of a Second Lieutenant and proceeded to serve in a highly decorated company of the Moroccan-based Spanish cavalry. With his inborn leadership skills, Franco quickly proved himself an able commander and rapidly rose through the officer's ranks. In 1915, he received the distinction of being the youngest captain in the Spanish army, and just five years later in 1920 he made the second in command of the prestigious Spanish Foreign Legion.

Three years later, Franco assumed full command and this was also when he got married. His wife Carmen Polo came from a distinguished Spanish family and the couple went on to have a daughter, also named Carmen, three years later.

Franco's able command of the Spanish Foreign Legion earned him admiration throughout the country. The Foreign Legion was a significant part of the Spanish armed forces and was exclusively responsible for maintaining Spain's colonial interests. With the effective suppression of Moroccan insurgency, Franco was hailed as a national hero and in 1926 was promoted to the rank of a brigadier general – he was just 33. Two years later, Franco was rewarded with the highly coveted appointment of the director of the General Military Academy in Saragossa. As part of his new duties, he started visiting military training establishments in Germany and

France; as a result he became acquainted with the cutting edge of military technology and the latest developments in military strategy, all of which he would go on to influence him to introduce military reforms in his own country.

Political Career

In the meantime though, major political changes were taking place in Spain. With the country fast spiraling into economic turmoil, Spain's King Alfonso XIII agreed to hold elections for the first time in sixty years. The people voted overwhelmingly against the decadent and ineffective monarchy and in favour of the Leftist Republican Party. The king, fearing further spread of dissent and turmoil in the country, fled Spain in April 1931.

The newly elected Spanish Republic consisted of Leftist political leaders and thus sidelined Franco, who was a known monarchist. Even though Franco was placed on the inactive list, he took the change in regime and his military prospects in stride. But before long another round of national elections was held in 1933 in which conservatives were voted into power. Franco's fortune seemed to be on the ascendant again – under the new dispensation, not only was his command reactivated but in 1934, he was further promoted to the rank of a major general.

In October 1934, Franco was called upon by the conservative government to crack down on an uprising of Austrian miners who had implicit support of the Left-wing Republican Party. Franco's success against the rebels turned him into a national hero and finally in 1935, he was promoted to the highest military rank of the Chief of Staff of the Spanish Army. Among his first military reforms was his insistence of rigorous discipline in the forces and strengthening of military institutions.

The political situation in Spain though, continued to remain on the boil. With many of the ministers of the conservative government being caught in scandals, protests broke out throughout the country. Fresh elections were ordered in February 1936 in which the Leftist Republicans were once again voted to power. However by this time, the political, economic and social structures had weakened so much, that all around there was confusion and anarchy. As Chief of Staff of the Spanish Army, Franco advised the new government to declare a state of emergency. But fearing him as a monarchist, the government took back Franco's Chief of Staff appointment and then removed him to serve at an insignificant post in the Canary Islands.

Rise to Power

Initially, Franco stayed away from any movement opposing the government. But as he watched the political system of his country disintegrate and with it, the social and economic structures come apart, he realized that he needed to take a stand. He swung into action upon receiving the news that the radical monarchist José Calvo Sotelo had been assassinated by the police. Finally on July 18, 1936, Franco announced a full military rebellion from his station at the Canary Islands. Under his leadership, the officers of the Spanish launched uprisings in multiple locations as a result of which Franco's forces assumed control of most of the western half of the country. His next step was to fly to Morocco with the intention of overseeing the transportation of troops to Spanish mainland.

As the rebellion gained strength, its leaders decided to choose a commander in chief. Francisco Franco was unanimously chosen as the supreme leader of the rebellion and on October 1, 1936, he became the head of state of the new Nationalist regime. The fight of the Nationalists to gain control of Madrid, where the remnants of the Leftist Republicans were ruling is known as the Spanish Civil War which continued for three years from 1936 to 1939.

Next Franco got busy in unifying all opponents of the Republicans on a common platform. He persuaded the Falange Espanola or the Fascists and the Carlists or monarchist supporters to come together and even got the culturally influential Catholic Church to support his rebellion. In order to further widen his support base, he sought out an alliance with the Italian dictator Mussolini as well as Nazi Germany in exchange for his support in the Second World War. This way Franco was able to secure arms and other kinds of resources that would vastly aid his chances against the faltering Republican forces.

Policies of Oppression

Though Franco was increasingly being seen as the only viable political alternative in Spain, his rise to political supremacy was not without force. Like any other dictator, he used harsh measures to wipe out political opponents and secure his own power. During the Spanish Civil War, as his forces marched northward to Madrid, they wreaked havoc on towns known for Republican majority. For instance in the town of Badajoz, fascist militia groups killed several hundreds of Republicans and their families. Later on, thousands of political prisoners would be executed by Nationalists before the blood-splattered Spanish Civil War would draw to a close.

Despite receiving military support from the Soviet Union and International Brigades, the Republicans were unable to hold out against the fierce onslaught Franco's men. The latter on the other hand were being aided by Italian Air Force and German military. As such in 1937, the Nationalists were able to regain control of Basque lands and Asturias. When Barcelona, the centre of Republican resistance, fell in January 1939, Spain realized that it was only a matter of time before the Nationalist assumed full power. That finally happened in March the same year when Madrid surrendered and April 1 marked Franco's full and unconditional victory.

Though the Spanish Civil War had come to an end with Franco's assumption of power, the reprisals against the Republicans continued. Thousands of Leftist supporters had already been killed or had fled to safer places, but even then Franco ordered special tribunals to be set up to try the remaining Republicans. These tribunals further sent thousands of Spanish people to the prison or to be executed. In fact in the mid-1940s, by Franco's own admission, Spain had some 26000 political prisoners. Moreover, trade unions were banned by law and the workers lost much of their rights that they had enjoyed during the Republican rule. Most importantly Franco ensured that a vast network of secret police was set in place that was asked to sniff out any hint of political opposition.

Along with the large-scale political repression, Franco's dictatorship had a cultural impact as well. Spaniards from the Basqùe and Catalan region were prohibited to speak their languages outside their homes. Catholicism was made the only acceptable religion and Franco went so far as to ban Basque and Catalan names for newborns.

Later Years

Having made an alliance with Axis Powers like Germany and Italy, Franco was compelled to take part in the Second World War, though he officially declared neutrality. Even then he ordered around 50,000 soldiers from his country to assist the German forces on the Soviet front. And though Tangiers was supposed to be administered internationally, Franco ordered the invasion of the Moroccan city. Also he allowed German submarines to use Spanish ports.

After the Second World War, Spain was sidelined in world politics for Franco's implicit support to the Axis Powers. But as Europe came under the shadow of the Cold War, Franco began to make overtures of friendship to the Western powers. Eventually in return for economic aid,

Franco agreed to let United States use Spanish soil for the construction of a naval base and three air bases.

Back at home, there was a growing clamor for return of monarchy. And since he had been a pro-monarchist in his military years, in 1947, Franco announced a referendum to bring back the king in Spain. However like any other dictator, he was careful to safeguard his own authority and declared himself as the lifelong regent of the state. The next year, Franco brought the ten year old Juan Carlos, the grandson of Spain's last ruling ruler, back to the country and began preparing him to be the future king of Spain.

In his last years, Franco modified many of the laws that were responsible for the worst excesses of his dictatorship. In 1943, Franco changed the identity of the state party, the Falange Espanola Tradicionalista, from a political organization to a 'movement'. This softened down the earlier fascist connotations of his party and his rule. Moreover, his unambiguous opposition to communist forces brought him closer to United States and in 1950, the United Nations finally invited Spain to become a member. Three years later, Spain under Franco also became part of NATO alliance.

The 1960s saw Spain make strides both in economic development and international diplomacy. Franco's bloody path to power was largely forgotten and he was now seen by the younger generation of Spaniards as an venerable statesman. As his health began failing during the 1960s, Franco announced that Prince Juan Carlos would succeed him as the head of the State and would preserve the essential structure of the government.

Finally on November 20, 1975, Franco died of a series of heart attacks.

Franco's Legacy

With almost thirty years of absolute power in Spain, General Franco turned out to be one of the longest reigning dictators of Europe. He steered the country through vastly troubling times, both in Spain and in the world. The fall of the Monarcy, the Spanish Civil War, the Second World War and successive changes of government were all negotiated under his astute iron-fisted leadership. This regime saw some of the most brutal force applied on political opposition and even cultural as well as religious pluralism was banned.

There were however some positive consequences of Franco's regime. For one, he brought about economic self-reliance to Spain and introduced modernization of the armed forces. Also, he managed to end the diplomatic isolation of Spain and by the mid-1950s, Spain was a member of both the UNO and NATO. By far the most significant benefit was the long period of government stability that his dictatorship brought about which not only paid economic dividends but ironically brought about a peaceful transformation to democracy.

After Franco's death in 1975, King Juan Carlos overturned many of the institutions of Franco's government. Political parties were legalized and just after two years of Franco's absence, national elections were held in Spain in 1977—for the first time in over forty years.

However in recent times, there have been events in Spain which point to an uncomfortable re-engagement with the country's past. The rise of extremist political groups playing up Franco's Nazi alliance, a growing political movement in Catalonia seeking freedom from Spain and in 2013, an Argentine judge's ruling about bringing some Franco-era security officials to justice for alleged crimes against humanity—all these have made the country question the complex nature of Franco's legacy.

For a long time, both the authorities and people of Spain were silent participants in the 'Pact of Forgetting', which kept quiet about the authoritarian nature of Franco's rule, so that the country's largely peaceful transition into democracy would be disturbed. But now with the economy on the brink of collapse and a fifty percent unemployment rate, there had been a churning in the political landscape too. Extremist right-wing groups were calling for a stricter government and limitations on the entry of foreign immigrants. Mostly, there has been an increase in the incidence of minor offences like extremist graffiti and workplace discrimination but scattered incidents like arson in a mosque and a racist killing of a man from Guinea have been in the news too.

One proof of the complexity of the issue at hand is the dissonance raised by a 2006 proposal from the Spanish government for legislation that will recognize the victims of the Franco regime. Known as the Law for the Recovery of the Historical Memory, this law would seek to compensate those who suffered under the dictatorship. However, the past is not an easy matter to resolve – while the majority Popular Party is reluctant to see a law that would open the wounds of the past, for the families of victims of the Franco regime it is important that the bodies in masses of unmarked graves are identified and relocated for reburial. Clearly, General Franco's legacy remains a mixed one in Spain.

□

Mao Zedong

D.O.B. – 26th Dec., 1893 Country – China
D.O.D. – 9th Sept., 1976

Among the principal figures of modern history, Mao Zedong is famous as the leader, who brought about the Cultural Revolution in the most populous country on the planet, China. Heading the Chinese Communist Party from 1935 until his death, Mao served as the chairman of the People's Republic of China from 1949 to 1959. But even after he relinquished the top post, he continued to be revered by the people as Chairman Mao.

Early Life

Born on December 26, 1893, Mao Zedong belonged to a family who had been farmers for several generations at Shaoshan, in the province of Hunan, China. Though most ordinary Chinese farmers led difficult lives at the time, Mao's father, being a grain trader, was better off as compared to others in his village. As such young Mao grew up in relative comfort. But while his mother was loving and supportive, Mao's father was a severe and authoritarian figure.

Mao's earliest education was in the village school where he did not learn much. In fact, by the age of thirteen, he was already working in the fields, the whole day as a result of which his education came to a standstill. In keeping with the social practices of the time in China, Mao's marriage was arranged, when he was just fourteen. But the young and increasingly restless boy refused to buckle under family pressure and rejected the marriage proposal. By this time, young Mao's desire to opt out of his village life and gain an education were getting increasingly stronger. When he turned seventeen, he gathered enough courage to leave home for Changsha, the capital of Hunan Province and there he got himself admitted to a secondary school.

Political Involvement

As Mao's geographical and social context changed, so too did his interests. He began to display a serious interest in the political issues of the day and deeply felt the social and economic wrongs borne by the ordinary Chinese. For centuries China had been ruled by monarchy which by the end of the nineteenth century had become decadent, incompetent and completely oblivious to the sufferings of the people.

Motivated by the urge to do something about the situation, Mao joined the Revolutionary Army and the Kuomintang, the Nationalist Party. In 1911 when the Xinhua Revolution broke out against the monarchy, Mao at saw this as an opportunity to bring about a change in the status quo and joined the Revolution. The Xinhua Revolution of 1911 was actually led by Chinese statesman Sun Yat-sen who motivated the Kuomingtan Party to overthrow the monarchy in China. In its place now the Republic of China was established.

After the Revolution, Mao went back to the Hunan First Normal School and finished his studies, passing out with a certificate in teaching in 1918. When he received news of his mother's death, he lost the last reason to go back to his village home. Instead he set off for Beijing, where he planned to take up a teaching job. But there was no teaching appointment available and he settled for the post of a librarian's assistant at the Beijing University and even attended a few classes in his spare time.

Greater exposure in the capital city as well as in a university allowed Mao to follow political trends in the rest of the world. He got to know of the Russian Revolution, which had overthrown the monarchy in Russia and in its place had established the Communist Soviet Union. Mao dreamt of something similar for China so that centuries of social and economic inequalities could be righted and China could have a new political order. As such in 1921 Mao Zedong along with some other activists established the Chinese Communist Party.

Though Mao Zedong had earlier joined the Kuomintang Party, he now found it easier to express his political ideals through the policies of Chinese Communist Party. Around this time, Mao became increasingly hooked to Leninist ideology which advocated the complete abolition of the class system and under the influence of Lenin, Mao too began to take up the cause of the poor peasantry in China. This in turn gave a fillip to the fortunes Chinese Communist Party which began to expand its influence as well as membership across the length and breadth of China. Even Kuomingtan leader Sun Yat-sen was able to read the mood on the ground and ordered his party workers to follow a policy of co-operation with the Chinese Communist Party. Though Mao Zedong had started his association with the Chinese Communist Party as one of the founders and then as an assemblyman delegate, he swiftly rose through the ranks until he became part of the executive to the Shanghai branch of the Chinese Communist Party.

Conflict with Kuomintang

In March 1925, Chinese President Sun Yat-sen died and was succeeded by Chiang Kai-shek who also assumed the position of the Chairman of the Kuomintang Party. Kai-shek was different from his predecessor as being more conventional and authoritarian. He did not see eye to eye with the Chinese Communist Party and not surprisingly was determined to crush Mao's growing power in Chinese national politics.

In April 1927, Chiang Kai-shek announced that there would no longer be any co-operation between the Kuomintang Party and the Chinese Communist Party. With the breaking of the earlier alliance, Kai-shek ordered a purge of the communists as a part of which many activists and even casual supporters were rounded up and imprisoned or worse killed.

Mao Zedong tried to fight back and in September, the same year, raised an army of peasants and set about from the countryside to Kai-shek's headquarters. However, Mao's army was promptly crushed and the soldiers who managed to escape death fled to Jiangxi Province, where they went about regrouping themselves.

In the hilly Jiangxi province, where Kai-shek's forces found it difficult to patrol regularly, Mao set about establishing his own political order. He was thus elected as chairman of the small republic. He gathered a small but lethal army of guerilla fighters. But while Mao was decisive in the way he initiated forward looking policies in China, much like a dictator he became increasingly intolerant of any political opposition. Thus, any dissident, who was different from Mao in government or party policies was quickly identified, imprisonment, tortured and then executed.

By 1934, the influence of Chinese Communist Party had widened to around ten regions in the Jiangxi Province. This increasingly became a cause for worry for Chiang Kai-shek, who realized skirmishes and small raids on outlying Communist strongholds throughout the country was not having the planned effect – that of discouraging people to join or support the Communist Party. Instead Kai-shek felt that nothing short of a large-scale attack would cow down the Communist Party. Accordingly, in October 1934, Chiang gathered together almost one million government forces and surrounded the Communist base town. This led to a flurry of tempers at the Chinese Communist Party as the leaders debated what to do. While a section of leaders advocated engaging the government forces in a do-or-die battle, Mao came up with the voice of reason. He advised retreat so that his party members could live to fight for another day.

Long Walk to Freedom

Thus from October 1934 and over a period of twelve long months, around hundred thousand Communists and their families left their homes in Jiangxi Province and trudged northwards and westwards to escape the excesses of the Kuomintang party workers. This came to be known as the Long March to Freedom in the course of which Chinese Communist workers and supporters travelled some 8000 miles, crossing formidable physical features like mountains and swampland to arrive at Yanan, in northern China. Not surprisingly out of the original 100,000, who began the journey, only 30,000 managed to survive the hazardous trek.

Despite taking many lives, the Long Walk to Freedom, served to inspire the ordinary people in other parts of China to migrate to Hanan where they could live a life of freedom from the excesses of Kai-shek's forces. Above all, it expanded the influence and raised people's faith in Mao Zedong, who now began to be revered as the top leader in the country.

Rise to Power

In July 1937, China became the victim of Japanese military aggression. The Kuomintang forces started losing control over coastal regions of China and its most important cities. Chiang Kai-shek's leadership floundered and he was forced to escape to the capital in Nanking. From there he reached out to Mao Zedong promising truce and co-operation if he could receive military help from the Communist Party. Mao took upon himself to rally his Communist forces to fight the

Japanese and with some help from the Allied Powers, was able to drive away the foreign invaders.

Mao's military victory over the Japanese and political victory over Chiang Kai-shek now paved the way for him to rise to the position of supreme power in China. Though there was some interference by Western powers, particularly the United States who did not wish to see a Communist Party come to power in the world's most populous country, eventually Mao was able to assert his authority. Finally on October 1, 1949, Mao marched to the Tiananmen Square in Beijing and announced the birth of the People's Republic of China. In order to escape reprisal, Chiang Kai-shek and his followers left for the island of Taiwan, where they established the Republic of China.

Period of Reforms

After achieving absolute power in China, Mao Zedong set about introducing sweeping reforms in the agricultural system, which most revolved around land reorganization. Large estates belonging to the erstwhile war-lords and the nobility were taken over by the government and broken up into agricultural communes where farmers could live and work on an equitable basis.

Mao Zedong also initiated a several measures to bring about social reform in the highly traditional Chinese society. Women were given the same legal status as men, education was thrown open to masses and literacy rate shot up. Also health care was made accessible to more people than ever before which insignificantly raised life expectancy rate in China.

While Mao's reforms brought betterment the life of the rural poor, who had for centuries struggled under economic and social inequality. Urban dwellers were less impressed by their leader's policies. There was growing discontent against Mao's high-handedness in imposing reforms and more about the coercive methods, sometimes his government used. He tried to address the problem by launching the 'Hundred Flowers Campaign' in 1956. As a part of this, people in cities were invited to express their objections and concerns in a democratic manner. However, when Mao witnessed the intensity of people's anger and opposition, his stance hardened and he overthrew any pretence of democracy. Mao's reaction was swift and severe – instead of allowing any more space for evaluation, he ruthlessly crushed every form of dissent. Hundreds of members of the urban intelligentsia and the civil society were arrested, imprisoned and even executed.

The Great Leap Forward

But far more infamous was The Great Leap Forward, an initiative conceived and launched by Mao Zedong with the ostensible purpose of increasing industrial and agricultural production. Under this plan, traditional small farms gave way to large agricultural communes in which as many as 75,000 people lived and worked on the fields. Each peasant family was supposed to get a share of the profit made by the entire commune and also own a small plot of land. Though well-intended, this plan of agricultural reform was too ambitious and did not take into account centuries of traditional farming methods and rural culture.

Worse still the initiative had no plan in place to cope with natural disasters. Thus, when the land was ravaged for three years by floods and bad harvests, food production plummeted and famine set in. This led to one of the worst man-made disasters in the human history with an estimated 40 million people dying of starvation between 1959 and 1961. Entire villages were wiped out. The horrific scale of the human tragedy was largely hidden from the ordinary Chinese citizens and neither did the world get to know about it. Even the figures for industrial production were exorbitantly inflated and fed to the people of the country. In fact, according to the historical sources, only high ranking

Communist Party leaders were aware of the extent of the tragedy and the inner coterie of Mao's supporters did not see the necessity of letting their leader know what was really going in the country.

Though the people were too crushed by starvation and famine to rise in revolt against the ill-considered Great Leap Forward, the abject failure of the initiative would have other consequences. For the first time in his life, Mao found himself pushed to the margins of the political landscape in his country. He realized that he no longer had a say in the central leadership and instead saw his rivals exercising supreme power.

Cultural Revolution

However, Mao had not been the supreme leader of China for decades without learning a thing or two about politics. He thought up a plan to return to power and in keeping with the tried and tested methods of dictators, created a national crisis, to which only he would provide the answers. And this was the germ of the Cultural Revolution. During his brief exile from power centre, some of Mao's writings were compiled by devoted supporter, Lin Bao, and turned into a handbook, titled, *Quotations from Chairman Mao*. Copies of the memoir were distributed amongst all Chinese and it came to be popular as the "Little Red Book". This was the start that Mao was seeking.

Once he was back in public memory, he made a dramatic appearance. In 1966, the 75-year-old Mao was seen swimming in the Yangtze River – then much was made about his superior health and fitness. The prime target of his stage managed appearance was the youth of the country who would not know much about the horrors of the Great Leap Forward. In keeping with them, Mao and his supporters orchestrated a series of public rallies which played up Mao's popularity among the young men and women of the country.

The next step was to spread rumours of supposedly right-wing plot in which the bourgeoisie were secretly planning to overthrow the communist government and bring back capitalist system. As had been the plan all along, the Chinese youth was easily swayed by such fears and Mao used them to man the Cultural Revolution by forming massive groups of 'Red Guards'. Educational institutions like schools, colleges and universities were shut down and the intelligentsia were punished with forced labour and sent to the countryside, ostensibly to be "re-educated" through hard manual work. Laws were passed ordering the destruction of all traditional arts and crafts. All around there was an atmosphere of economic and social chaos throughout the country. Not surprisingly in September 1967, as many cities edged closer to a state of anarchy, Mao ordered the army to step in and restore order. Amidst all this, only one thing stood out with clarity—Mao was back in supreme control of the country.

Like all dictators, Mao could not be satisfied with absolute power in his own country but hankered for international influence as well. Consequently, in 1972, Mao pushed for a meeting with the then President of United States, Richard Nixon. The meeting not only cooled down the fires of antagonism between the two countries but more importantly for Mao, established him as the leader of a country whose time in world politics had finally come.

On September 18, 1976, at the age of 82, Mao Zedong died from complications arising out of Parkinson's disease.

Mao's Legacy

Though Mao Zedong was instrumental in freeing China from the crippling chaos of Kuomintang government, especially in the wake of Japanese invasion, there is no doubt that this stability was achieved at great cost to its people. Millions of people lost their lives while agriculture and industry suffered repeated blows as a result of his skewed Great Leap Forward policy.

Then like all dictatorial regimes, Mao's rule was marked by widespread human rights abuses; dissenters were routinely arrested, imprisoned without trial and even executed. This sort of excess was even formalized in the laws passed during the Cultural Revolution which was responsible for the death of one-and-a-half million people throughout the country and struck a death blow to the traditional artistic and cultural heritage of China.

Among the positive aspects of his legacy was Mao's insistence on the self-reliance of China. Though agricultural and industrial reforms took time to come into effect, eventually China became economically self-sufficient. So by the time of Mao died, the China that he left behind was a far cry from the poor and weak nation of late nineteenth century. Mao had led his country to economic and strategic importance, though in the process, his countrymen had paid a very high price.

□

Josep Broz Tito

D.O.B. – 7th May, 1892
D.O.D. – 4th May, 1980

Country – Croatia
(Yougoslavia)

Josep Broz, later famous as Marshal Tito, was a leader of Yugoslavia and served as the head of the country in various positions from 1943 till 1980. Tito was not only highly respected at home for his reforms and his unification initiatives but also held in great regard in the international community for his refusal to become part of either the Western capitalist or the Eastern Soviet bloc. Marshal Tito was one of the most important leaders of the NAM or Non-Aligned Movement which maintained equal distance from both superpowers, the USA and USSR, during the Cold War. Tito is one of the rare powerful diplomats of twentieth century whose legacy is seen in more of a positive than negative light.

Early Life

Born on 7 May 1892 in Kumrovec, in the northern Croatian region of then Austro-Hungarian Empire, Josep Broz was the seventh child of peasant couple, Franjo and Marija Broz. As a child, Broz spent many years in the Slovenian village of Podsreda where he was in the care of his maternal grandfather Martin Javersek. In 1900, the young Broz was enrolled in a primary school at Kumrovec and graduated in 1905.

Two years later, in 1907, Broz left behind his rural life and headed for Sisak where he got a job as an apprentice to a machinist. It was during this time that he was first exposed to politics of the day and gravitated towards the labour movement, eventually joining the union of metallurgy workers. In 1910, he formally became a member of the Social-Democratic Party of Croatia and Slavonia. For the next three years, Broz worked as a mechanist and travelled through many of the industrial cities in Austro-Hungarian Empire.

First World War

With the clouds of the First World War building up on the horizon of Europe, Broz signed up in the Austro-Hungarian Army in 1913. After graduating from a training institute for non-commissioned officers, he was posted to the 25th Croatian Regiment based in Zagreb in the rank of a sergeant. Though skilled and courageous, Broz had a mind of his own from the very beginning. In 1914, he won a bronze medal at an army fencing competition in Budapest. But when the First World War broke out the same year, he angered his superiors by engaging in anti-war propaganda for which he was even arrested and imprisoned in the Petrovaradin fortress.

In January 1915, with the Austro-Hungarian army locked in war against the Allied Forces, Broz received orders to head for the Eastern Front in Galicia where a battle was raging against the Russians. Here too, Broz proved his courage and skill on the battlefield, for which he was promoted to the rank of Sergeant Major, becoming the youngest soldier to hold that position in the Austro-Hungarian Army. However, his victorious run soon came to an end after he was wounded at Bukovina and captured by the Russian forces on 25 March 1915.

Involvement in Communism

Broz remained a prisoner of war for a long time during which he was sent to the Ural Mountains to work at a labour camp. Here he got to know the Bolsheviks and started taking an active interest in their political movement. This proved fortuitous for him as an insurrection by the miners in 1917 led to an attack on the prison in which Broz managed to escape. He next travelled to St. Petersburg where the Bolshevik Revolution was in full swing after which he joined the Red Army. However, the October Revolution and its aftermath proved to be violent times during which Broz was again imprisoned. After escaping once more, he made for Kirgiziya and then returned to Omsk, where he married his Russian fiancée, Pelagija Belousova. In the spring of 1918, he joined the Yugoslav section of the Russian Communist Party. However, the responsibilities of a family compelled Broz to look for work and for a short while he found employment as a mechanic near Omsk.

Return to Yugoslavia

By the end of 1919, Broz had had enough of roaming across Russia and early next year, he decided to return to his home country with his wife. In September 1920, Broz came back to Croatia which was now part of the Kingdom of Serbs, Croats and Slovenes. One of the first things he did upon his return was to become a formal member of Communist Party of Yugoslavia (CPY). However, the group was soon slapped with a state ban which in turn drove its political activities underground. Because of his links to the more radical elements of the Communist Party, Broz was perpetually under state surveillance and could not find steady employment.

However, Broz fared better in his party responsibilities. He quickly rose through the party leadership – having started out on a local level of the CPY, Broz found himself in the position of organizational secretary for the CPY committee that was in-charge of Zagreb. All this impressed the Communist Party heads in Moscow and Broz was rewarded with the position of the political secretary of the

CPY. Once again Broz proved his leadership skills which were evident in the way he energized the party members and took the lead in planning and organizing demonstrations throughout the city.

But all this was still dangerous under the political dispensation of Yugoslavia so in 1928, Broz was arrested and imprisoned, on charges of stocking bombs at his house.

It would be March 1934, before Broz found himself a free man again and he marked this event by changing his name to Tito. Soon after, he left for Vienna where he received a warm welcome by the CPY leadership and even an invitation to join the ruling Politburo.

Next Tito travelled to Russia where he escaped by the skin of his teeth when it became evident that a wave of violence was being launched at many revolutionaries of foreign origin. Upon returning to Yugoslavia, Tito appeared to be helping Stalin to subjugate rebellious forces; so not surprisingly when the purge was over, Tito was given the leading position in the party and in 1937, and he took charge of the Central Committee.

The Second World War

During the time, when Tito was made top leader of CPY, the Second World War broke out in Europe. In order to keep the Axis Powers at bay, Tito organized some of his communist followers into a resistance group who came to be known as the Partizans. One of the most effective resistance groups in Europe, the Partizans not only fought to push back the Axis Powers but even seized control of the region that the invading forces had captured initially. By 1943, it was evident that Tito was a name to reckon with among the anti-Axis groups in Europe and at least in Yugoslavia, he was the primary force behind the resistance activity. So next year when the exiled royals of Yugoslavia expressed their wish to return to the country, it was with Tito that they engaged in a series of negotiations. But all said and done,

Tito was an ardent communist and when the Second World War headed to an end from 1944 onwards, he declared the CPY as the ruling party of the country and with it became the nation's absolute leader.

Domestic Rule

Like all dictators, Tito was also determined to wipe out all political opposition in his country. As such, from mid-1945 till the year's end, he engaged in a fearful programme of political repression. All those opposing communism and especially Tito's leadership of Communist Party of Yugoslavia were identified and either arrested and imprisoned or executed. In order to give a semblance of legitimacy to his rule, Tito ordered the holding of fresh elections which were then completely rigged. Eventually, Tito renamed the country as Communist Federal People's Republic of Yugoslavia. Though these measures often abused human rights and undermined political opposition, in the end it helped Yugoslavia to suppress nationalist insurrections and remain a united country, something that would unravel in the decades succeeding Tito's death.

However with time and knowledge that his rule was secure, Tito ordered many reformist measures in Yugoslavia. In the latter half of the 1960s, policies were put in place to encourage private enterprise. Many restrictions on freedom of speech as well as religious expression that had been imposed earlier were now relaxed. On 1 January 1967, Yugoslavia became the first communist country to abolish visa requirements, thus throwing open its borders to all foreign visitors – an unbelievable step at the peak of the Cold War.

In 1971, Tito was elected as the President of Yugoslavia by the Federal Assembly for the sixth consecutive time. He used this occasion to introduce as many as twenty wide ranging amendments to the constitution. These were aimed at decentralizing governance and granting greater autonomy to republics and provinces. It was decided that the federal government would be the higher authority only in supremely important matters like defence, foreign affairs, internal security and finance with a responsibility towards encouraging free trade within Yugoslavia and furthering loans to underdeveloped regions. All policies and initiatives related to education, healthcare and housing would be determined by the governments of the respective republics and the autonomous provinces. Another amendment provided for a rotating presidency, albeit which would come into effect after Tito's own death. A new constitution was passed in 1974 also which aimed to equalize the smaller states with the larger two. However, most of these measures required a very delicate balancing act – something which Tito's successors were unable to continue and eventually resulted in the eruption of nationalist insurrections.

International Relations

Though Tito ascended the political throne in Yugoslavia with the help of the Soviets, soon he showed his desire to take an independent line. The Soviet interferences in Greece and Albania were used to demonstrate its intrusive nature and then justify Yugoslavia's breaking away from the influence of the communist superpower. Above all, Tito proved to be far more charismatic than Stalin which in turn fuelled the breach between the two leaders. Driven to desperation, Stalin attempted to bully Yugoslavia into accepting Soviet ascendency but Tito refused to be cowed down. He continued to command the unswerving loyalty over the country's army, government and police went a long way in making Tito confident enough to stand up against the Soviet leader. So even when the rest of Eastern Europe was firmly in the grip of Soviet influence, Yugoslavia was the only nation to maintain an independent stance vis-à-vis USSR.

For a brief while in the late 1940s, Tito flirted with the idea of an alliance with Western capitalist countries, mainly to obtain American aid from the Economic Cooperation Administration (ECA). However, Stalin's death in 1953, brought a shift in Tito's plans and he once again encouraged proximity with the Soviet bloc. The result was that Yugoslavia qualified for aid from the COMECON as well. In this way, Tito kept experimenting with the possibility of alliances with each side – something which was easily facilitated by the antagonism between the Western capitalist and Eastern Soviet bloc.

Eventually though, Tito decided to adopt a policy of equal distance from both superpowers which developed into the Non-Aligned Movement. With partners such as India's Jawaharlal Nehru, Egypt's Gamal Abdel Nasser, Indonesia's Sukarno and Ghana's Kwame Nkrumah, Tito took the lead in a opening up a third alternative for countries who did not want to get sucked into the conflict between the two superpowers of the Cold War. The non-aligned states held their first meeting in Belgrade in 1961 and on 1 September 1961, Tito became the first Secretary-General of the Non-Aligned Movement. This initiative heightened Yugoslavia's prestige on the international scene and raised Tito's reputation as a world leader.

Last Years

After 1974, Tito concerned himself less and less with matters of daily governance. He was more interested in appearing as the elder statesman of the country rather than the face of the government. This on one hand served to build a personality cult revolving around the forever popular leader of the people, while at the same time allowing him to escape the uncomfortable consequences of the very policies that he had put in place – like the students' rebellion of the late sixties with which Tito apparently sided and which was eventually blamed on the government.

Tito began to remain unwell from 1979 onwards. In January 1980, he was admitted to hospital and was treated for a host of medical problems for the next few months till he finally died on May 4, 1980, just three days before his 88th birthday, but still the dictator of Yugoslavia.

Legacy

Marshal Tito as he came to be popular in the world is acknowledged as one of the rare dictators in modern history who has left behind a mostly positive legacy. He managed to unify all the provinces of Yugoslavia so that it remained a single entity under his rule. From 1970s, he even ushered in decentralization of the government so that regional aspirations could be addressed. He has been credited with creating the best living conditions in a communist state of the time.

However, according to some critics, these achievements were not without their costs. The highly centralized and harsh political measures that Tito initially used to ensure the country's unity often used instruments of political repression and cultural domination. Even though later Tito brought in constitutional amendments to decentralize governance, the purge of political opponents that he accompanied this which played a significant role in Yugoslavia's eventual disintegration. Historians have pointed out that if Tito had not replaced liberal reformers with centralists and hardliners, then the road to reform may have been smoother and not wracked by insurrections and ethnic conflicts.

In the end though, Tito's greatest success seems to have been in his stature as a world leader. He was one of the rare communist leaders to follow an independent foreign policy, without succumbing to Soviet influence. And because of its neutrality, Yugoslavia would often be an exception among communist countries to have diplomatic relations with some right-wing, anti-communist governments too. Over all, the Non-aligned Movement helped Tito to earn respect on the world stage and made international powers take Yugoslavia seriously.

□

Leonid Brezhnev

D.O.B. – 19th Dec., 1906 Country – Ukraine
D.O.D. – 10th Nov., 1982

Leonid Brezhnev was a Soviet leader who held sway over the government for almost two decades from 1964 until his death in 1982. Though he was part of the three-member committee that ruled USSR in that period, effectively all power resided in him. Today Brezhnev is best remembered for improving USSR's relations with the United States but also for pushing his own ideology in both domestic and international relations of the country.

Early Life

Born on December 12, 1906, Leonid Illyich Brezhnev came from a working class background in Kamenskoye, an industrial town in the Ukraine that is now known as Dneprodzerzhinsk. His family had worked in the steel mills for several generations and his father Ilya Yakovlevich Brezhnev had followed the same profession. Brezhnev's mother was Natalya Denisovna, who tried her best to bring up their three children amidst difficult living conditions.

Apart from economic hardships, Brezhnev witnessed extended political turmoil during the time he was growing up. The First World War broke upon Europe in 1914 and raged till 1918. Closer home, Brezhnev and his family suffered the uncertainty of civil war in Ukraine and also felt the effects of the Russian Revolution in 1917.

At the mere age of fifteen, Brezhnev had to take up a part-time job at a trade school, where he helped in the work of a land surveyor. After graduating from school in 1923, he enrolled at the metallurgical institute in Kamenskoye and at the same time he joined the Communist Party of the Soviet Union (CPSU) in 1931. After graduating in 1935, Brezhnev worked for a brief while as an engineer and was even appointed as the director of a technical institute. However, he was more interested in a political career, to further which, he held a variety of party posts.

At the time Joseph Stalin was at the helm of affairs in Soviet Union and Brezhnev was careful to remain in the dictator's good books. In keeping with harsh communist policies, Stalin ordered the peasants of the country to sell their extra grain to the state rather than keeping it for themselves. Brezhnev, in his role of party member, played an active role in enforcing these policies, often going to the extent of using violence and coercion against the farmers to get them to obey the state diktat. Later he would deal with political opposition in a similar manner, like, ordering the arrest and imprisonment of the scientist Andrei Sakharov for speaking out in favour of human rights and against nuclear weapons.

By 1939, Brezhnev had succeeded to the post of the secretary of the regional party committee of Dnepropetrovsk. The outbreak of the Second World War saw Brezhnev join the Red Army as a political commissar. Among his chief responsibilities, was the Russification of diverse parts of the Soviet Union. This was a pet ideology of Stalin which aimed at bringing cultural and in the process political uniformity in the entire population. For instance, children in traditionally non-Russian parts of the Soviet Union were forced to study Russian subjects in school. Likewise newspapers across USSR were ordered to be printed in the Russian language only.

By dint of hard work and political connections, Brezhnev quickly rose through the military ranks until in 1943 he was made a major general in the Red Army. At the same time he was given the leadership of political commissars on the Ukrainian front.

After the close of the Second World War, Brezhnev left the Army in 1946. Now he could devote his entire attention to his political career in which he rose from strength to strength. 1950 marked an important year in his political journey, when he was elected to first secretary of the Central Committee of the Moldavian SSR, which was one of the states that had been conquered by USSR and made part of the Soviet Union. In Moldovia, Brezhnev's main brief was to enforce the Russian culture on the indigenous population who were primarily Romanians. After staying for two years in Moldovia, Brezhnev returned to Moscow. He was now made part of the influential Secretariat of the Central Committee of the Communist Party and got an opportunity to personally serve under Joseph Stalin.

However, the Soviet dictator's sudden death brought Brezhnev's rising political graph to a halt. Because he was seen as a Stalin loyalist, Brezhnev in absence of his mentor, had to give up his appointments on the Central Committee as well as in the Politburo. Instead he had to be satisfied with the relatively insignificant position of deputy head of the political department of the Ministry of Defence and carry on with the rank of lieutenant general. In 1954, he was sent to the Kazakh Republic as the second secretary of the Kazakhstan Communist Party.

At the time, Nikita Khrushchev was the head of the Secretariat and the *de facto* ruler of the entire Soviet Union. Brezhnev worked hard to prove his worth to the new leadership and actively implemented Khrushchev's Virgin and Idle Lands Campaign in Kazakhstan. In recognition of his efforts, Brezhnev was soon promoted to first secretary of the Kazakhstan Communist Party in 1955.

Eventually though, ruling members of Central Committee realized that a party leader like Brezhnev with superior administrative skills would be more of a boon than a threat and in 1956, he was called back to Moscow with an appointment in the Secretariat. He was re-elected to his posts on the CPSU Central Committee and in the Politburo. During this time, Brezhnev also once again proved himself a loyal soldier of the reigning leader by undermining the rebellious efforts of the 'antiparty group' that was determined to topple Khrushchev. In gratitude, Khrushchev approved of the former's appointment as the chairman of the Presidium of the Supreme Soviet.

Rise to Power

Though the Chairman of the Presidium of the Supreme Soviet was a prestigious position and made him the titular head of the Soviet Union, it did not exercise any real power. And so after three years, Brezhnev resigned from that post to become Khrushchev's assistant as second secretary of the Central Committee. By this time, he was considered the potential successor to Khrushchev. But Brezhnev was not ready to wait till Khrushchev would willingly make way for the next leader. So after returning to the Secretariat Brezhnev began looking for opportunities to strengthen his own position. One of the ways was to ally himself with senior party members who were opposed to Khrushchev's policies or influence.

By the end1964, Brezhnev had managed to put together a coalition of leaders opposed to Khrushchev which eventually forced Khrushchev to abdicate his leadership of the Central Committee. In the arrangement that followed, Brezhnev took on the position of the first secretary of the party's Central Committee which, like Khrushchev before him, made him the *de facto* ruler of the entire Soviet Union.

In 1966, Brezhnev adopted the title of the General Secretary of the party's Central Committee. Since this was the same title under which Stalin had ruled USSR, it was evident that Brezhnev was planning to rise still further in the government. Initially though, he seemed content to govern as one of the three members of "collective leadership", the other two being Premier Aleksey Kosygin who was designated the chairman of the Council of Ministers and Nikolay V. Podgorny, appointed the chairman of the Presidium of the Supreme Soviet.

Eventually, Brezhnev did away with the formality of the post-Khrushchev three-member arrangement. He had already taken on, in 1976, the appointment of the Marshal of the Soviet Union which made him the only party member after Stalin to assume the highest military rank in the country. The very next year in May, he relieved Podgorny from the position as chairman of the Presidium of the Supreme Soviet and within the next month, he had already been elected to that position. With this, Brezhnev became the first individual in the history of Soviet Union to hold the leadership of the party and of the state at the same time. Brezhnev now was the supreme leader of the entire USSR and his control over the government as well as the party was complete.

Foreign Policy

Brezhnev in some ways was different from other dictators before him; while leaders like Lenin and Stalin crushed any political opposition with whatever force necessary, Brezhnev left internal affairs of the state to his colleagues of the 'collective leadership'. Likewise matters of domestic economic development as well as relations with non-communist state were delegated to others. What interested Brezhnev most were military affairs and foreign relations.

One of the highlights of his foreign policy was something known as the Brezhnev Doctrine under which Soviet Union claimed the right to intervene in the internal politics of a country when "the essential common interests of other socialist countries are threatened by one of their number." The most notorious implementation of this doctrine was the invasion of Czechoslovakia in 1968. In between 1967 and 1968, Alexander Dubcek tried to dilute the communist system in Czechoslovakia and usher in a measure of liberalism. However, this was strongly opposed by Soviet Union and members of the Warsaw Pact. Thus led by Brezhnev, the Soviet Bloc sent its forces into Czechoslovakia and forced Dubcek to resign as First Secretary in April 1969.

The Brezhnev Doctrine not only heightened tensions with countries of the Eastern Bloc, but also with some Asian communist nations, like China. In 1969, relations between two of the largest communist countries in the world were strained by the Sino-Soviet border conflict. The Chinese demanded that USSR cut down its military presence in the Sino-Soviet border, withdraw its troops from Afghanistan and the Mongolian People's Republic as well as extend support to Vietnam for its invasion of Cambodia. It would be more than ten years before Brezhnev would call for normalization of relations with China during his May 1982 speech in Tashkent.

The biggest misadventure prompted by the Brezhnev Doctrine was perhaps the Soviet invasion of Afghanistan in December 1979. The 1978 revolution of Afghanistan had brought to power a communist government which soon proved it authoritarian and intolerant of its people's real wishes. When Soviet Union saw the communist government in Afghanistan in danger, it sent its armed forces into the country and thus started another long episode of conflict and bloodshed in the region.

While most of his foreign policy initiatives were directed by the Brezhnev Doctrine, in the 1970s, though Brezhnev sought to normalize relations between the Soviet Bloc and the Western powers, particular the United States. Relations between the two super powers had started to thaw since the time of Khrushchev. Thus, the Partial Test Ban Treaty was signed in 1963, the Helsinki Accords in 1975 and both countries agreed on the installation of the red telephone line between the White House and the Kremlin. However under Brezhnev, the easing of the relations between Soviet Union and the United States known as the détente covered wider and more comprehensive ground, including not only matters of arms race and military build-up but also East-West trade, the security situation in Europe as well as human rights.

Brezhnev went on to develop a cordial relation with the US President Richard Nixon. The two leaders visited each other more than once and among the real consequences of this policy of détente were a large purchase of American wheat by the Soviet Government as well as the creation of a joint United States-Soviet space program in 1975. In 1979, Brezhnev reached agreement with US President Jimmy Carter on a new bilateral strategic arms limitation treaty popularly known as SALT II, but the US Senate refused to ratify the treaty. One of the last foreign actions taken under Brezhnev's leadership was the intervention in Poland. In the early 1980s, Poland saw the rise of the solidarity mass movement, which harnessed much of the public dissent against the Communist Polish Government. Though initially Brezhnev seemed to be in favour of letting Poland thrash out is internal problems, with the law and order situation worsening in the country, the Polish military leader Wojciech Jaruzelski imposed a state of war and was supported by Moscow in his actions.

Apart from foreign relations, the other aspect of government that interested Brezhnev was the development of the Soviet military. Under Brezhnev, the USSR continued with its status of having the largest army in the world but at the same time ensured that its navy was accorded a large arsenal of the latest technology. In fact, Brezhnev made sure that the Soviets were equal to the Americans in strategic nuclear weapons, and because of all the investment in the military-industrial complex, the space programme of USSR soon overtook that of America. The Soviet astronauts and cosmonauts gave many firsts to the world, including the first human in space as well as the first woman in space.

Though the programme of military development and modernization launched by Brezhnev was heavily dependent on industrial expertise, this sector soon began to show signs of stagnation. In keeping with the communist ideology, the system of production, distribution, and even use of goods and services was all controlled by the state. Initially, this paid rich dividends in terms of national wealth and social equality, but eventually it led to an impasse in the economy and people losing on energy and creativity. There was too much uniformity everywhere and economic innovation and enterprise began to suffer.

Also because of high levels of military expenditure as well as restricted investment on light industry and consumer goods, the Soviet economy suffered from a slow-down in 1973. Likewise agriculture too was suffering. Production was just not enough to feed the population and gradually people began to raise voices against lop-sided economic policies that had been followed by many decades of communist government. Overall GNP growth rates of the Soviet Union began to fall in the 1970s and went past the mark that the country had experienced in the 1950s and 1960s; a matter of greater concern was that the Soviet growth rates had fallen even behind those of Western Europe and the United States.

Last Years

Faced with growing dissent among the East Bloc countries as well as worsening of the economic situation in

USSR, Brezhnev began keeping unwell since the end of the 1970s. Suffering from long-term health problems, Brezhnev finally died in Moscow on November 10, 1982.

Legacy

As the supreme leader of the Soviet Union, the chief achievement of Brezhnev was creating a strong military-industrial identity for the country as well as making USSR the leaders in space technology at the time. However, these developments came at a cost – they proved to be a big drain on the financial resources of the country, leading to slide in agricultural production, health and welfare services and this ultimately to the stagnation of the Soviet economy in mid-1970s. With his death, Brezhnev left the Soviet Union without any strong leadership until Mikhail Gorbachev emerged in the political landscape of the country in 1985.

□

Kim Il-Sung

D.O.B. – 15th April, 1912
D.O.D. – 8th July, 1994

Country – Korea

Kim Il-Sung was the first leader of North Korea in modern times who went on to establish a political system based on dictatorship by descendents of the Kim family. Kim Il-Sung not only liberated the country from Japanese occupation in the Second World War but set up a rigid communist state which was later changed to the lines of his own political ideology of Juste. He was the country's premier from 1948 to 1972 after which he became president of the country and remained so until his death on July 8, 1994.

Early Life

Kim Il-Sung was born as Kim Song-ju on April 15, 1912 in Mangyondae near Pyongyang, the capital city of North Korea. When Kim was still very young, his parents moved to Manchuria to escape the Japanese occupation. During his days in Manchuria, Kim learnt Chinese and joined a school to get an education. But while still a student, he signed up with a communist group and got involved in revolutionary activities which lead to his arrest and imprisonment in 1929-30.

After Kim got out from the prison, he took up the cause of Korean independence. In 1931, he joined the Chinese

Communist Party (CCP) for its ideology of anti-imperialism and as a way of getting back at the Japanese. His plans came nearer to fruition when in 1935, he was accepted the Northeast Anti-Japanese United Army, a guerrilla faction run by the Chinese Communists. Here Kim succeeded in impressing a senior officer, Wei Zhengmin who had the ear of the higher echelons of the CCP. As a result of this patronage, Kim managed to get the command of an army division of several hundred men and led them to a victory over Japanese forces, even briefly seizing a small town on the Korean/Chinese border. Though strategically, this feat did not have much importance in the long run, it succeeded in getting Kim noticed by his Chinese sponsors and earned him regard of the scattered band of Korean guerilla fighters. Kim thought it only fit to take on the title of a famous Korean guerilla fighter from the past, Il-Sung.

The brief victory that Kim managed over the Japanese forces had another consequence. With the Japanese army retaliating and pushing deeper into China, Kim and his men were forced to retreat back, crossing the Amur River and escaping into Siberia. Here they were given refuge by the Soviet agencies who arranged for Kim to obtain USSR for training in communist ideology as well as military strategy, especially guerilla tactics.

After arriving in the Soviet Union, Kim formally joined the Communist Party. He also signed up with the Red Army and in the rank of a major, led a Korean contingent in the Second World War. After the defeat of Japanese forces in the War and their eviction from Korea, the country came to be split between the opposing influences of United States in the southern part and Soviet Union in the northern part.

Rise to Power

It was during this time when Kim returned to Korea after being away for more than two decades. Immediately, he set about organizing a regional communist group known as People's Committee of North Korea and became its chairman – later the group would come to be known as People's Committee of North Korea. Eventually with the support of Soviet Union, Kim established a provisional government in the northern part of the country, now known as North Korea. In 1948, the country was formally named as Democratic People's Republic of Korea, with Kim as its premier.

The Korean War

Confident in his position as the absolute ruler of North Korea, Kim Il-Sung now began planning an invasion of South Korea with the aim of unifying the two halves under his own communist North Korean rule. Initially, his international allies, the Soviet dictator Joseph Stalin as well as the Chinese leader Mao Zedong, were doubtful of the feasibility of the invasion. But eventually lured by the idea of expansion of communist society as well as prospect of eviction of American influence from the region, the leaders of two major communist powers agreed to Kim's expansionist plan.

The result was the Korean War. On June 25, 1950, Kim ordered his forces to attack South Korea and within a span of just three months, the North Korean army had got the upper hand. The southern forces and their UN allies were pushed to the southern coast of the peninsula, called the Pusan Perimeter and it seemed that they had no option left but wait for a desperate defensive battle. Incredibly though, the South Korean army and its UN allies managed to get their act together and bear down upon the invading North Koreans till even the latter's capital city, Pyongyang, was in South Korean control.

At the impending fall of Pyongyang, the North Korean leaders including Kim Il-Sung escaped to China. With the UN forces in hot pursuit, Mao Zedong was forced to intervene and the Chinese Army successfully held back the

Allied Forces at the Yalu River. This was followed by months of bloody conflict until in December 1950, the Chinese Army recaptured Pyongyang from Allied control. The war on the whole, however dragged on well into 1953. In the middle of the year, it was clear that neither side was winning and the costs had begun to run too high. Thus, in July 1953, with no end to the stalemate, Korea was once again divided along the 38th Parallel. Though Kim Il-Sung once again took over the reins of the government in North Korea, the Korean War had effectively put an end to his ambition of reuniting the two Korean haves under North Korean rule.

Rule by an Iron Hand

The misadventure of the Korean War had cost North Korea a good deal. The country was in dire straits as far as the economy was concerned. Partly in order to get the economy back on track and partly to translate his communist utopian society into a reality, Kim ordered an extremely severe model of state control in every aspect of the economy. Thus, all private farms in the country were seized from individual owners and turned into collective farms on which agricultural workers labored like in factories.

Industry too was modeled according Kim's strictly communist ideas. The state owned all the factories now and the focus of industrial production was restricted to military weapons and heavy machinery. The immense expenditures on the manufacture of arms and military equipment further impoverished the state and were largely responsible for the successive famines that wracked North Korea in the later twentieth century.

To ensure that there was no opposition to his radical economic and political measures, Kim ordered a cultural propaganda. The dissemination of all information was controlled through the state – through all information channels, his own contribution in the Korean struggle against Japanese forces were exaggerated and at the same time, other agencies were accused of outlandish charges – like the UN were charged with spreading diseases among the North Korean people. Inexorably this led to a personality cult.

The other side of this kind of cultural propaganda was an extreme form of political repression. Any political rival or even party dissident who dared to speak out against Kim's policies disappeared overnight without evidence of any formal legal process like an arrest, trial and defence. Often entire families of a protesting individual would be taken away by the secret police, never to be seen again. This kind of swift and brutal action ensured that all citizens, party workers and also members of the government remained silent and completely acquiescent to all that the decisions that were taken by the North Korean dictator.

Relations with Soviet Union

Though Kim Il-Sung had sought the help of USSR and China during his fight against Japanese occupation and later against South Korea and its allies, relations between North Korea and the powerful communist states did not always run smooth.

Kim had always been an ardent supporter of Joseph Stalin and had liberally sprinkled his speeches in North Korea with glowing references to the Soviet dictator. But with Stalin's death, there began a shift of allegiance between North Korea and USSR. Nikita Khrushchev became the next absolute leader of USSR and began a policy of de-Stalinization. Also Kim did not trust Khrushchev as he thought the latter's reforms were against the communist ideology.

The growing rift between Khrushchev and Kim came out into the open when the North Korean leader sided with China in the Sino-Soviet Split of 1960-89. Kim ordered the expunging of any reference to his Red Army stint from his official biography and as a way of highlighting his anti-

Khrushchev stance, put in place extreme Stalinist policies in the North Korean government.

The rift with Khrushchev's Soviet rule had another consequence for Kim. With the relaxing of Stalinist allegiance in USSR, criticisms against the former Soviet leader's policies were now increasingly heard. This in turn encouraged some quarters of North Korean government to voice their own apprehensions against Kim and his policies. Though at first Kim seemed uncertain on how to deal with these criticisms, eventually he fell back on his old repressive measures and ordered yet another purge. A large number of dissidents were executed and many more were driven to flee the country.

Relations with China

Though Kim inched closer to China in order to offset his suspicions of a Khrushchev-led Soviet Union, relations with the northern communist neighbor were not smooth sailing either. Mao Zedong had extended useful support to Kim in the past, especially in the Korean War but now the aging Chinese leader seemed to be losing his influence in the government. By launching the Cultural Revolution of 1967, Zedong tried to make himself relevant again but to Kim this seemed to bring about nothing but instability and confusion. Moreover, Kim was worried that such a step might influence a similar state of chaos in North Korea as well. Thus, Kim lost no time in denouncing the Chinese Cultural Revolution, claiming that it had brought about incoherence into a carefully planned communist society. At this volte-face from an ally, Mao Zedong reacted sharply – he ordered information propaganda against Kim Il-Sung and later began sending out feelers to the United States too for a better understanding between China and America.

Having found both the USSR and China to be unreliable allies, Kim now began exploring East European communist countries for opportunities of international support.

The main among these were East Germany where Erich Honecker was in power as well as Romania which was ruled by another feared dictator, Nikolai Ceausescu.

Towards the middle of 1960s, Kim started seeking inspiration from Ho Chi-Minh for his near-successful efforts in reuniting North and South Vietnam. Impressed by the Vietnamese leader's use of guerilla warfare in the Vietnamese struggle for independence from French colonial government as well as in the Vietnam War, Kim began planning subversive activities in South Korea too. As part of this policy, Kim okayed the assassination attempt of South Korean President Park Chung-Hee according to which a 31-member North Korean special forces unit was sent to Seoul in January 1968 and even got within 800 meters of the Blue House or the South Korean presidential residence, before being stopped by South Korean police. Again the same year, North Korea captured the crew of the spy ship USS *Pueblo* and in general raised its conflict level with South Korea and the US in the demilitarized zone.

Doctrine of Juste

With both China and USSR turning out to be difficult allies, Kim Il-Sung now decided to follow a policy of self-reliance or Juste. According to this, people of North Korea were exhorted to fall back upon their own resources, whether in the economy, governance or in defence of their country. Kim declared that North Korea would no longer act as a satellite state of either the USSR or China and forge its own internal and foreign policies.

The ideology of Juste though seemingly noble in theory, was impractical to the extreme. It only resulted in greater suffering for the people of North Korea as well as further turmoil for the economy. Despite frequent famines, Kim refused all international aid so as to publicly be seen as following the policy of Juste.

In order to enforce such extreme policies, it was important for Kim to be seen as the unopposed leader of the nation and this was brought about by an elaborately constructed personality cult. In 1972, he declared himself as the President of North Korea. The people of the country were repeatedly told that Kim was the "Sun of the Nation" and could do no wrong.

Increasing Isolation

From 1980s onwards, North Korea found itself increasingly isolated on the international front. His erstwhile allies, USSR and China, were themselves going through significant changes. In 1979, then Chinese leader, Deng Xioping introduced important economic reforms which took the country further away from the past communist policy of strict state-control on all economic activity. With a measured opening up of the market, China no longer felt the need to engage with the stagnating North Korean economy.

The Eastern Bloc of communist states on the other hand was now a thing of the past. From 1989 to 1991, east European countries like Poland, Czechoslovakia and Romania had overthrown their communist governments. But most importantly the Soviet Union had disintegrated to give way to newly-independent political entities. All this left North Korea one of the last few rigidly communist states. Except for limited trade and contacts with China, Russia, Vietnam and Cuba, North Korea was practically cut off from the world.

Kim's continued refusal to introduce any kind of reform in the economy or political system had also played its part in North Korea's international isolation and had left it to sink into economic turmoil. The ideology of Juste had failed miserably and had only passed on the burden of monstrous military expenditures on an already fragile agricultural system. All this resulted in successive famines but Kim remained resolute in refusing international aid.

Things only got worse when Kim, fearing energy shortage due to a crumbling economy, started a programme of nuclear research and development. The wariness of Western countries and UN increased and there were also threats of international sanctions against North Korea. Finally in June 1994, former US President Jimmy Carter flew to Pyongyang to persuade Kim to stop his nuclear program and incredibly enough, the North Korean leader agreed to a meeting.

However before any anti-nuclear agreement could take shape, Kim Il-Sung suddenly died of a heart attack, on July 8, 1994. His son Kim Jong-il took over the government, as had already been decided by Kim Il-Sung in the succession policy of 1980.

Legacy

During the nearly five decades that Kim Il-Sung was in power, he not only succeeded in isolating North Korea from all reformist and democratic influences of the world but established one of the most powerful personality cults of all times which has continued even after his death. Thus while communist dictatorships pass from one powerful party leader to another, Kim Il-Sung was able to establish a line of succession along his own family.

Though Kim Jong-il became the dictator of North Korea after his father, he never took on the title of the 'President' and instead came to be known as the 'Dear Leader' of the country. Because of his father's succession policy, Kim Jong-il became the world's first leader of a communist state to inherit power. He continued with his father's ambitious policy of militarization of North Korea and in the process, pushed his country-people further into famine and starvation. At the same time, Kim Jong-il carried on with his aggressive nuclear policy and for many years took no notice of the ban imposed by United Nations on the development of nuclear arsenal and long range ballistic missile testing. However, in December 2011, Kin Jong-il sent diplomats to Beijing to negotiate a deal with the US according to which, he would give certain concessions on nuclear development in return for food aid for the starving North Korean populace. But before any agreement could be finalized, Kim Jong-il died from an apparent heart-attack, thus leaving the country's future course of nuclear action uncertain.

Kim Jong-il was succeeded by his youngest son, Kim Jong-un, who has reportedly declared to continue his country's policy of nuclear testing and even development of missile technology. However, Kim Jong-un appears to be more media aware than his predecessors and has also, on other occasions, claimed to devote more of the country's resources on educational and economic reforms, including a contentious policy which would allow North Koreans to work in China. In a departure from his father and grandfather, Kim Jong-un has also been seen to adopt certain 'Western interests' – there have been reports in the media of him giving a New Year's broadcast, accompanying American player Dennis Rodman to a baseball match and even enjoying a public musical performance with his wife.

Thus the hereditary line of dictators established by Kim Il-Sung seems secure for now. Though the present ruler Kim Jong-un seems more open to Western cultural influences, politically there are no signs of encouraging democracy in North Korea. And finally Kim Il-Sung's lasting importance to North Korea can be estimated from the fact that despite his grandson Kim Jong-un being the *de facto* ruler now, Kim Il-Sung continues to be referred to as the Eternal President of North Korea. Massive statues and portraits of Kim Il-Sung can be seem throughout the country and at the Kumsusan Palace of the Sun in Pyongyang, his embalmed body rests in a glass coffin for all to see and pay their respects.

□

Nicolae Ceausescu

D.O.B. – 26th Jan., 1918
D.O.D. – 25th Dec., 1989

Country – Romania

Nikolae Ceausescu was a communist leader and dictator who ruled Romania for more than two decades. During this time, Ceausescu was the absolute authority in the country and in fact his reign came to be considered as one of the harshest in the entire Eastern Bloc of the Cold War. Though Ceausescu came to power as an elected leader and began his rule with a relatively balanced government, over time, he became brutally repressive and exploitive. His tyrannical rule came to an end in 1989 when a popular insurrection led his deposition and the former dictator was finally executed with his wife on the orders of a Romanian court.

Early Life

Born on January 26, 1918 in the small, rural town of Scornicesti, just outside of Bucharest, Nikolai Ceausescu came from a humble background. His parents had ten children and as such they were able to afford only an elementary education for young Nikolai. When only eleven, he was sent to work at a Bucharest factory so that his family could make ends meet. This kind of deprivation from early childhood left a lasting impression on Ceausescu and in 1932, even before he turned eighteen, he decided to join the workers' movement which was taking shape in Romania.

Ceausescu proved himself a committed worker to the cause of Romania's labour movement and by the mid-1930s, he had made a name for himself in the country's Union of Communist Youth. However, radical communist politics was banned in the country at the time which is why Ceausescu's involvement in underground communist politics led to his arrest followed by an imprisonment of thirty months.

In 1939, during a brief reprieve, Ceausescu married Elena Petrescu who was also a communist activist.

In 1940, Ceausescu was sent back to prison which however turned out to have unforeseen benefits. When behind bars, his cell-mate turned out to be no other than the famous Romanian Communist leader Gheorghe Gheorghiu-Dej, who would eventually become the top statesman of the country and form his own government in 1952. During their prison term, Ceausescu picked up Marxist-Lenin theories from Gheorghiu-Dej and benefitted from the patronage of the senior communist leader who introduced to other senior party members in Bucharest.

With the weakening of the Axis Powers in the Second World War and the arrival of Soviet troops, Ceausescu managed to escape from prison in August 1944. This was a time of great political instability in Romania which the Soviet Union would take advantage of and occupy the country. Initially, the Communist rule as established by the Soviet forces in Romania proved to be advantageous to Ceausescu. He quickly rose through the ranks in the Romanian army, becoming a brigadier general in 1945.

With the Communists acquiring full power in Romania in 1947, Ceausescu's former cell-mate and mentor Gheorghiu-Dej became the top ruler of Romania by the end of 1940s. Hence, Ceausescu came to occupy extremely important positions both in Romania's communist party as well as in the government. From 1948-50, he headed the ministry of agriculture and then from 1950 to 1954 he served as deputy minister of the armed forces in the rank of major general.

In 1955, Ceausescu was invited into the party's Politburo – the most important decision-making body of the Communist Party. Here too, it was only a matter of time before Ceausescu had grasped the most powerful appointments so that by the end of the decade he was supervising the party's organization structure as well as overseeing the cadres. Thus, it did not come as a surprise when just before his death from cancer in 1965, Gheorghiu-Dej anointed Ceausescu as his successor.

Initially, Ceausescu was appointed as the First Secretary of the party, which came to be known as the General Secretary from July 1965. And then he was appointed the President of the State Council from December 1967, which effectively made Ceausescu the head of state in Romania.

Initial Liberalism

The initial years of Ceausescu's rule were rather moderate and some historians would say even liberal, both in domestic and foreign policy. In fact, he was one of the first leaders of the Soviet Bloc to reach out to Western leaders at the height of the Cold War and came to be seen as a reform-minded communist. He travelled extensively across the world, meeting foreign dignitaries and in 1969, even invited the newly elected US President Richard Nixon to Romania. At the same time, Ceausescu saw to it that Romania also shared good relations with its traditional communist allies like China. Back at home, he even eased press censorship in the 1960s.

Ceausescu's main aim in building good relations with other countries was to highlight Romania's independence vis-à-vis Soviet domination of the Eastern Bloc. Ceausescu wanted to be seen by his countrymen and by the world as the author of a nationalist, independent foreign policy that did not blindly adhere to orders issued from Moscow. Thus for the most part of the 1960s, Ceausescu distanced himself from the interventionist policies of the Warsaw Pact military alliance. Most significantly, he condemned the 1968 invasion of Czechoslovakia by members of the Warsaw Pact. Once again a decade later, he spoke out against Moscow's invasion of Afghanistan in 1979.

Iron Rule

Such independent initiatives in foreign policy were part of a carefully laid out plan according to which Ceausescu intended to cement his position as the supreme ruler of Romania. Tapping in the popular sentiment against Soviet domination, Ceausescu came up with his own political ideology, which was a mix of communism and strict nationalism. This was expressed most clearly in his July Theses, which marked a clear turnabout from his earlier quasi-liberalism to a narrower, harsher political ideology, according to which the party and nation were supreme. Strict ideological conformity was to be complied in all walks of life, whether in arts, culture, humanities or technology.

Even personal and family life was not spared of state control. Contraception was banned and divorce made difficult with the aim of swelling the population of Romania. But instead of leading to addition of many more families, such policies only ended up in huge increase of numbers of abandoned babies and overcrowded orphanages.

Initially, Ceausescu buttressed this policy with an ambitious economic program which focused on extensive industrial and agricultural development. Thus, the 1960s and early 1970s were projected in official discourse as a time of nation building in which all Romanians had a duty to participate and contribute.

Eventually though, Ceausescu's real agenda of absolute and lasting power became clearer. His grip on political and economic situation grew tighter; by following a ruthless policy of political repression and secret policing, he ensured that there remained no opponents, whether in the party structure or in the government. There was no free speech, the citizens and the media were perpetually under police surveillance and the slightest hint of dissent was brutally crushed by arrest, imprisonment and even execution.

All this was accompanied by an elaborately constructed personality cult – Ceausescu was praised as in the official media. His wife and other family members were appointed in the highest posts of the party as well as the government. Finally in 1974, Ceausescu declared himself as the President of Romania. Though he was already the president of the State Council since 1965 and thus the *de facto* ruler of the country, yet he did not possess any titular supremacy and was one among other members of the State Council. His actual power resided in his position as party leader. But with him assuming a full-fledged executive presidency in 1974, Ceausescu was now the leader, both in name and action.

His Downfall

However, it was Ceausescu's economic policies which would eventually hasten his downfall. He ordered in massive building projects and industrial ventures in the 1970s, which proved too expensive for the small country. By 1980s, the nation's treasury was almost depleted and foreign debt had swelled to unmanageable proportions. With a view to pay off this debt, in 1982, Ceausescu ordered the export of the country's agricultural and industrial production. Though this slashed the foreign debt of Romania by half, it also had an imaginable impact on the lives of the ordinary Romanians. Overnight, there was acute crisis of the basic necessities like food, fuel, energy and medicines; standard of living fell to such levels that Romania came to be counted among the poorest countries of Europe. Even when one of the world's largest socialist states, the Soviet Union, embarked on a program of economic liberalization – led by Mikhail Gorbachev's policies of perestroika and glasnost – Ceausescu continued to exercise excessively rigid state control of the economy. Not surprisingly, people began to let out their frustrations and sufferings in the form of demonstrations all across the country. Things rapidly spun out of control when Ceausescu announced that rural settlements of less than two thousand people would be razed to the ground to make way for large agro-industrial centers. In November 1987, the Communist Party headquarters in Brasov became the scene of a violent agitation in which thousands of workers stormed the building, destroyed records and even demolished a portrait of Ceausescu. Images of uprisings, which could not have even been imagined a few years back were not being played out in different parts of the country.

Matters came to a head on December 17, 1989 when Ceausescu ordered his security forces to fire on a group of people demonstrating against the government in the city of Timisoara. As news of the brutal firing spread, violent protests by the people began erupting in the capital city of Bucharest. On December 22, the army turned its back on the Romanian dictator and decided to stand by the popular uprising of the people. This proved to be the last straw and prompted Ceausescu to try and escape with his wife. However, the couple was captured before their helicopter could leave the country and was taken into custody by the armed forces.

As Romania sank deeper into violence and chaos, the new government wasted no time in bringing Ceausescu to justice. On December 24, in a show trial that lasted less than an hour, the former dictator and his wife were convicted on charges of genocide and other crimes. Soon after the court read out the sentencing, Ceausescu and his wife were led outside and executed by a firing squad. Ceausescu and his wife were buried at the Ghencea Cemetery in Bucharest.

His Legacy

Though Ceausescu came in power as a forward-looking Communist leader, according to some historians, he in fact turned out to be one of the most repressive in the history of the modern world. The extent of police surveillance and state control over all institutions that existed in Romania under Ceausescu can perhaps be only compared to the strictest years of Stalin rule in former Soviet Union.

If political repression and ideological conformity were some of the harshest aspects of Ceausescu's rule, the other was surely his economic policies. Forced to pay for garangutan building projects and wasteful extravagances of the ruling elite, ordinary Romanians sank deeper and deeper into poverty and misery. The most visible reminder of this remains the ironically-named People's Palace – an enormous building measuring 3.77 million square feet, that drove the country into foreign debt, demanded the demolishing of 19 churches, six synagogues and 30,000 homes and still remained unfinished at the time of the dictator's death. It boasts some of the most luxurious fittings in the world and is today considered the second biggest building on earth after the Pentagon. Currently, it houses the Parliament of Romania, the Constitutional Court but also plays host to some of the most high profile celebrity events in this part of the continent.

But the rare glamorous symbol of Ceausescu's rule aside, the legacy of the dictator has largely been difficult. Romania has still not been able to fully emerge from the consequences of twenty-five years of economic exploitation of its resources. Overcrowded children's homes and a low quality of life as compared to European standards remain other aspects of the dictator's legacy of harsh social rules. In the end, however the people's power remained triumphant even though the uprising of 1989 left more than thousand civilians dead and Romania turned out to be the only country to experience violence in the wave of revolutions that swept communists from power across Eastern Europe twenty years ago.

□

Pol Pot

D.O.B. – 19th May, 1925 Country – Combodia
D.O.D. – 15th April, 1998

Pol Pot was the leader of a Cambodian communist party known as Khmer Rouge, which ruled the country from 1975 to 1979. Though Pol Pot ruled for a relatively lesser time as compared to many other dictators of the world, his reign was one of the most brutal in modern history. His policies and attempts to create a rural, communist society led to the deaths of one and a half million people in Cambodia – a veritable genocide which has been immortalized in global popular culture with black and white images of mountains of skull and bones. Known as the Killing Fields of Cambodia, these bear testimony to the brutality of just four years of Pol Pot's rule. Though the dictator died in 1998, he was never brought to justice for the horrendous crimes against his own countrymen.

Early Life

Born as Saloth Sar on 19 May, 1925 in a place called Kompong Thong province in central Cambodia, Pol Pot was lucky to be born to the parents from relatively successful background as they owned roughly fifty acres of land growing rice paddy, which was around ten times the national average. At the time, Cambodia was a French

Protectorate and Pol Pot's family could afford to have him educated in a series of French-speaking schools.

In 1934, Pol Pot left for the Cambodian capital city of Phnom Penh, and here he spent a year at a Buddhist monastery. Next he shifted to a French Catholic school, where he received a well-grounded education. In 1949, he qualified for a scholarship and went to Paris for higher education, his chosen subject being radio technology. It was here in Paris that Pol Pot was first exposed to communist ideas and joined a few militant political groups.

Political Activism

Pol Pot returned to Cambodia in 1953. This was a time when the movement from French colonial rule was at its strongest and there were several nationalist parties fighting for Cambodian independence. Pol Pot joined one which advocated the setting up of a Communist society, the Khmer People's Revolutionary Party (KPRP). The KPRP was founded in 1951 with help from North Vietnamese government which was strongly communist and favoured the same political orientation in neighbouring countries.

In the next ten years, Pol Pot played an active role in the organization of the KPRP, giving it a distinct Marxist-Leninist direction. Though ostensibly, he continued to work as a teacher, instructing students in French literature, history and geography, in reality he began planning for ways to bring about a communist revolution in the society. After the French colonial government withdrew from Cambodia, the country went back to the monarchy system and was ruled by Prince Norodom Sihanouk. Being a communist party, the Khmer Rouge was completely against the monarchy and thus under Pol Pot it began plotting to change the political system in the country.

In 1963, the government authorities in Cambodia initiated a crackdown on communist rebels. As a result, Pol Pot and other Khmer Rouge activists had to flee to the remote regions of the country. Initially, they encamped with members of the Viet Cong, another strongly communist organization from South Vietnam that fought a bloody guerilla war against the US and the South Vietnamese government during the Vietnam War 1959–75. This support proved useful to Pol Pot who emerged as the leader of the Khmer Rouge party and raised a guerilla army with the intention of launching attacks on the forces of the Cambodian Government. The guerillas started their campaign by first bringing the relatively thinly populated northeastern part of the country under their control.

Meanwhile important political changes were taking place in the capital city, Pnom Penh. Under the monarchy system that returned with the liberation of Cambodia from colonial France, Prince Norodom Sihanouk was the ruler of the country. But his reign was weak and taking advantage of the Prince's visit outside the country, a military coup led by General Lon Nol deposed the monarchy in March 1970.

But instead of bringing about a clear change of government, the military coup plunged Cambodia in civil war. Prince Sihanouk allied himself with the Khmer Rouge party while General No l sought the help of United States and two sides entered a long campaign marked by military violence but most of all by the use of atrocities in unarmed civilian population.

Worst of all, Cambodia was drawn into the Vietnam War – around 70,000 American soldiers as well as South Vietnamese forces crossed into its borders to fight the Viet Cong and North Vietnamese soldiers who were in Cambodia during the war. Now having become the theatre of war, Cambodia was made the target of a secret bombing mission by US President Richard Nixon. As part of this, no less than 500,000 tons of bombs were dropped on Cambodia by American planes within a span of four years.

All this brought a tremendous amount of suffering for the people of Cambodia. But for Pol Pot, the war time action of the Vietnam War afforded him an opportunity to increase his power. More and more recruits began joining the Khmer Rouge party with the help of which it was able to expand its area of influence. In fact, by the time the Vietnam War ended in 1973, the Khmer Rouge had brought almost three-fourths of Cambodian territory under its control.

Having seized control over most of the country, Pol Pot now had the capital city as its target. Phnom Penh was subject to heavy shelling with artillery and rockets. Though the city was full of refugees, the Khmer Rouge went ahead with its plan of bombarding the city. In 1975, the rebels destroyed the airport and put in blockades at river crossings. Finally in April 1975, the Khmer Rouge forces entered the capital city seized control of the government with this; Pol Pot was now the most powerful man in Cambodia.

Though Pol Pot had been able to bring Cambodia under Communist rule, the human costs were immense. The bombings and blockades of Phnom Penh had resulted in the death of thousands of people due to starvation and suffering. Despite an American plane trying to airlift supplies, it just wasn't enough and by the time the Khmer Rouge had established its control over the city, at least half a million lives had been lost in the Civil War.

Brutal Regime

Influenced by a combination of Marxism and Leninism, Pol Pot began forcing his own version of communism on his countrymen. He wanted an entirely new social order based on rural communism – towards this ostensible end, he forced all residents of Phnom Penh to vacate the city and forced them to go to the countryside to work on fields. The main targets of this policy of forced labour were intellectuals, academicians, civil servants, professionals and city entrepreneurs – people who would be able to see through his repressive policies and organize some sort of protest.

The party took over all private property in the city and sent the owners to villages as part of the 're-education' process which in fact turned out to be a human disaster of huge proportions. People were forced to work under the harshest conditions – often without adequate food, water, clothing, shelter and healthcare. Even if anyone who survived the inhuman conditions could still fall prey to the most brutal of working conditions. Men, women and children were made to slave in the fields and anyone who complained or concealed rations would be sent to the detention centre for interrogation and torture. Among these centres, the S-12 became infamous for unimaginable atrocities carried out on helpless people and for executing thousands of forced labourers.

Extreme Reforms

With Phnom Penh in their control, Pol Pot ordered his party to introduce reforms based on his version of communism. One of the most immediate changes took place in agriculture – privately owned fields were taken over so that farms could be collectivized under state control. People were not only banned from owning any property privately, but even forbidden from keeping money or jewellery.

Pol Pot's so-called reforms far exceeded the economic sphere and sought to control almost all aspects of people's lives. Any form of religion was outlawed and most reading material was forbidden. Only books and newspapers approved by the state were allowed to any form of circulation in the country. Not only public lives, but Khmer Rouge under the hawkish leadership of Pol Pot went so far as to control the private lives of people – thus the government laid down rules regularizing language, dress codes and sexual relationships, as well. Anyone found flouting the rules – whether at home or in public place – was arrested and punished severely.

Pol Pot's dictatorial influence was evident from the way he sought to change the symbolic identity of the country too – thus the Khmer Rouge ordered that Cambodia would be henceforth known as Democratic Kampuchea. In an extreme manifestation of this megalomania, Pol Pot ordered Khmer Rouge to re-align even the rice fields of the country so that the symmetrical checkerboard which existed on their coat of arms could be depicted on the fields.

Fall from Power

The dictator whose rise to power had been phenomenal and whose exercise of that power had sent millions to their death was not destined to reign for long. After seizing control of Phnom Penh in April 1975, Pol Pot forced Prince Sihanouk to resign which he assumed the office of the Prime Minster of the country in 1976. But though Khmer Rouge had defeated the combined forces of Prince Sihanouk and the US, its own people had got embroiled in the fight with the Vietnamese. By 1976, border conflicts between Cambodia and Vietnam were growing in frequency as well as intensity. In 1977, the fighting accelerated and in December 1978, the Vietnamese government was forced to push in a sizeable army contingent across the border into Cambodia. This contingent included 60,000 armed soldiers as well as artillery guns and equipment for air attack. The invasion proceeded from the border, liberating villages and towns on the way from Khmer Rouge control till on January 7, 1979, the Vietnamese army took control of the capital city. Pol Pot was compelled to leave Phnom Penh and once again escape to the thick jungles beyond the countryside. From here, over the next few months, he rallied his forces and started guerrilla warfare against the government forces.

Though the Khmer Rouge was now considerably weakened, it was not yet finished. The geopolitics of the region had ensured that the super powers of the world had some stake in keeping the party alive. Thus, Pol Pot and his party continued to receive arms and ammunition from China through the 1980s on ideological grounds.

Interestingly, even the capitalist United States offered some kind of political support to Khmer Rouge since the former was worried about the occupation of Cambodia by the Vietnamese which would continue for ten years.

In 1991, however an agreement was reached between main guerrilla factions and Vietnam-backed new Cambodian government according to which a ceasefire would be put in place. By the end of the decade, Pol Pot's influence was almost depleted as the Khmer Rouge had practically lost all relevance in the politics of the time. Also the party itself was being divided into many smaller factions and in 1997, one of these captured Pol Pot. The former dictator who had passed so many orders for imprisonment, torture and killings was now himself under house arrest.

On April 15, 1998, Pol Pot suffered a heart attack and died in his sleep.

Legacy

Pol Pot left behind a legacy of inconceivable brutality in which an estimated one to three million people died out of a population of slightly over eight million. In effect, his policies had wiped out around 25% of the total population of the country either directly by torture and execution or indirectly by illness and starvation. He came to be known as the Butcher of Cambodia and the presence of mass graves hastily dug to dispose of bodies of men, women and children, led to the moniker, Killing Fields of Cambodia.

Even after losing his power within only three years and being under house arrest for over a year, Pol Pot remained unaccountable for his crimes till the end. Not a single country of the world or the United Nations could bring him to trial for his role in ordering the genocide against his own country people. Till today, after one and a half decades of his death, only a handful of Khmer Rouge officials have faced trial on charges of humanity.

□

Fidel Castro

D.O.B. – 13th August, 1926 Country – Cuba

Fidel Castro is best known to the world as setting up the first communist state in the western hemisphere and having brought the US on the brink of a nuclear face-off during the Cuban Missile Crisis in the Cold War period. Castro ruled Cuba from 1959 when he overthrew Batista to 2008, when he made way for his younger brother Raul. During these five long decades, Castro's regime ushered in many social and economic reforms for the poor of Cuba but many international observers alleged that the period also saw widespread human rights violation in Cuba. While the overall effect of Castro's regime remains open for discussion, there is little doubt about the fact that this dictator from Cuba not only changed the course of his country's history but had a decisive impact on global politics.

Early Years

Born as Fidel Alejandro Castro Ruz on August 13, 1926, Castro was the third of six children. He had two other brothers named Raul and Ramon as well as three sisters, Angelita, Emma and Augustina. Castro was born near Birán, in Cuba's eastern Oriente Province. His father Angel was of Spanish origin but had made good as a sugar plantation owner in Cuba. His first wife was Maria Luisa Argota to whom Castro's mother Lina Ruz Gonzalez, had been a maid. It was only when Castro was fifteen, that Angel dissolved his first marriage and took Lina Ruz as his wife. A couple of years later, Castro now a seventeen year old young man, received formal recognition as Angel's son.

Growing up in a family of wealthy plantation owner, Castro received the best of educational facilities. Initially, he went to private Jesuit boarding schools, after which he enrolled in the El Colegio de Belen, where he turned out to be more interested in sports rather than studies and was consequently a sought-after pitcher of the school's baseball team. Castro graduated towards the end of 1945, following which he signed up for the law course at the University of Havana.

Political Activism

While studying law at the University of Havana, Castro became involved in the political questions of the day. Though coming from a wealthy family himself, he was distressed at the economic hardships of the ordinary Cubans. Castro seethed at the widespread economic disparity among Cubans according to which people like plantation owners and foreign industrialists enjoyed immense wealth and economic power while the workers in fields and factories labored under the harshest conditions.

Not surprisingly, Castro's anti-imperialist and nationalist affiliations began taking on socialist colours. He was not only passionate about the betterment of social and economic conditions in Cuba but in other neighbouring countries as well. In 1947 thus Castro set off for Dominican Republic with the idea of joining forces with rebels opposed to the rule of Dominican leader Rafael Trujillo. However, the coup turned out to be a failure and Castro was forced to return to his country.

Opposition to Batista

The failed coup attempt though was not able to dampen

Castro's socialist and reformist fire and soon he found another cause to champion. After his return to the University of Havana, Castro began working for an anticommunist political party named Partido Ortodoxo. This party was founded by Cuban presidential candidate Eduardo Chibas with the primary aim of tackling deep-rooted corruption in the government which was mainly responsible for the misery of the ordinary Cubans. Among other ideals of the party were social reform as well as economic and legal freedom from foreign influence, especially the American industrialists.

However, Castro and his political fortunes received a jolt in 1948 elections in which Chibas lost. Three years later in 1951, Chibas once again considered running for the presidential elections but found himself isolated as erstwhile members of his party refused to support his allegations of government corruption. In the meantime, former president general Fulgencio Batista, continued to make headway on the national political stage. Chibas tried to warn the people of Batista's ruthless and corrupt practices but could not rally support for his political beliefs. Disillusioned, Chibas shot himself during a radio broadcast and thus effectively brought to an end, any hope for a democratically elected government in Cuba.

In the meantime, Castro got married to a woman named Mirta Diaz Balart, with whom he had a child too, named Fidelito. However, any personal happiness in his life proved short-lived because of his political ambitions. During the national elections of 1952, Castro tried to contest a seat in the Cuban Parliament. But a coup led by General Batista toppled the government and resulted in the cancellation of the election. Castro not only found his political aspirations crushed but even his economic circumstances were badly hit. In the end, the marriage could not survive the demands of Castro's political involvement and was dissolved in 1955.

As soon as Batista seized power, he went about solidifying his own position and rooting out all opposition. He not only managed to get the support of the economic and military elite of Cuba but even convinced the United States to legitimize his regime. There was only a meager opposition, led by some members of the Partido Ortodoxo among which Castro was prominent figure. "From that moment on, I had a clear idea of the struggle ahead," he said in a 2006 "spoken autobiography." In an attempt to overthrow Batista, Castro organized an insurrection according to which around 150 Partido members launched an attack on the Moncada military barracks on July 26, 1953. But the attack turned out to be a failure and ended with capture of Castro as well as some of his other compatriots. During the trial, Castro was convicted and sentenced to fifteen years in prison.

Association with Guevera

Though the insurrection against Batista could not achieve its end. Castro's conviction and incarceration led to an outpouring of huge support from all parts of the country. Castro became famous throughout Cuba as the strongest voice against the corruption and excesses of the Batista regime. Partly under such popular pressure, the Batista government was forced to strike an amnesty deal in 1955 according to which Castro was freed from prison.

After his release, Castro left for Mexico where he planned to meet the dynamic revolutionary leader Ernesto Che Guevera. Driven by the plight of the poor of Latin American countries, Guevera believed that the only way social and economic justice could be brought about was by guerilla warfare. This system of political action Castro was impressed by Guevara's political philosophy and came to the conclusion that guerilla warfare was the only way to address the political situation in his homeland. Consequently, Castro and Guevera joined hands and decided to return to Cuba.

On December 2, 1956, Castro with 81 supporters landed on the eastern city of Manzanillo with the aim of launching an attack on Batista's forces. However, the ill-prepared insurgents were roundly defeated by Batista's soldiers. Fortunately for Castro, he along with his brother Raul and Guevara were able to evade the soldiers and make their way into the refuge provided by the thickly forested Sierra Maestra mountain range which lay along the island's southeastern coast. Though Castro and his people had escaped with their lives, they were now faced with new challenges as there was virtually no weapons or supplies they could fall back upon.

Castro's Guerilla Warfare

Castro however did not give up his dreams of overthrowing the Batista regime. Even when hiding in the mountains, the revolutionaries started reorganizing with only two rifles. Gradually by early 1957, the insurgents were launching small attacks on the Rural Guard patrols of the Batista government and even winning local recruits on to their side. "We'd take out the men in front, attack the center, and then ambush the rear when it started retreating, in the terrain we'd chosen," Castro would go on to recount later in his 'spoken autobiography'.

In this way, Castro's supporters waged a guerrilla war against the Batista government from 1956 to 1958. During this period, Castro was able to organize small resistance groups in towns and villages across the country. As a measure of growing popular support, Castro was even able to run a parallel government of sorts in the regions under his control. There was some attempt at bringing in agrarian reform and regulate agricultural and manufacturing production.

To a great extent, Castro's increasing political influence was the direct result of the misrule of the Batista regime. Farm and factory workers were now fed up with the economic burden imposed on them by the corrupt and extravagant Batista government and even in the military, there were large-scale desertions in the lower ranks. Castro realized that the time was right to launch an offensive and from 1958, he ordered a series of military strikes against the government forces throughout Cuba. His military campaign was successful and the insurgents were able to capture and hold significant cities and areas of the country. In January 1959, Batista was forced to flee to the Dominican Republic, leaving the political stage open for Castro. At the mere age of 32, Castro had succeeded in conducting a classic guerrilla campaign against a powerful general and national leader, and had finally taken control of Cuba.

Castro Gains Supreme Power

After overthrowing Batista, Castro was welcomed into Havana by cheering crowds. He set up a new government with Jose Miro Cardona as prime minister while Castro himself assumed the position of commander-in-chief of Cuba's armed forces. Even United States extended its recognition of the new government. When Cardona unexpectedly resigned in 1959, Castro took over as the country's prime minister – by now his ascension to supreme power was complete.

One of the first things Castro did upon ascending to power was to usher in a series of social and economic reforms. He ordered that factories and plantations be nationalized, partly in order to limit American influence on the economy of Cuba. As part of these reforms in May 1959, Castro brought into effect the First Agrarian Reform Law, which restricted the size of land holdings and banned foreigners from owning property in Cuba. Though the overt aim of such land reforms was to form a class of independent farmers, in effect it brought farms under state control on which farmers were mere government employees.

Soon there were other signs of uneasiness with Castro's extreme reforms which the Cuban leader dealt with firm swiftly and harshly. There were growing accounts of purges in the military services as well as silencing of any media critical of Castro's policies. By the end of 1959, it was clear that Castro's revolution had been radicalized and that he had effectively became a dictator.

Castro and his Anti-American Stance

Castro's overtly socialist reforms inevitably brought him closer to then Soviet Union. In February 1960, Castro established diplomatic relations with USSR and also signed a trade agreement according to which Cuba would buy oil from the superpower. This brought about a swift reaction from the United States; part of this reprisal, American-owned refineries in Cuba refused to process the Soviet oil. Cuba retaliated by seizing the refineries and the US in turn slashed Cuba's import quota on sugar. American interests had already been hit by Castro's nationalization drive and especially when Castro refused to pay compensation according to prevailing property rates and instead based it on the exceedingly low prices that the companies had manipulated the past Cuban governments into agreeing with so that they would have to pay minimum taxes.

Now with USSR entering the picture, America hardened its anti-Cuba stance. On January 3, 1961, outgoing President Dwight Eisenhower terminated diplomatic relations with the Cuban government. In April the same year, Castro formally declared Cuba to be a socialist state.

The next day US government launched a covert mission against Castro according to which 1,400 Cuban exiles, having been trained and armed by the Central Intelligence Agency, were asked to land at the Bay of Pigs and from there organised an attack to overthrow Castro's regime. The insurrection proved to be a massive failure – hundreds of the insurgents were killed and another thousand were captured. Though for many years, the United States denied any involvement, later de-classified records showed that the insurrection was planned as early as October 1959 under the Eisenhower administration and was carried out under the Kennedy government.

Far from overthrowing his regime, the Bay of Pigs incident actually strengthened Castro's position. Playing on fears to his life, he attacked American imperialism and declared the end of democratic process in Cuba. Furthermore, he formally declared himself to be a Marxist-Leninist and announced a slew of measures that were firmly coloured with communist ideologies. On February 7, 1962, the United States hit back by imposing full economic embargo on Cuba, a policy that remains in effect toil this day.

The Cuban Missile Crisis

As part of Castro's increasing reliance on the Soviet Union, Cuba continued to welcome military and economic aid to Cuba. In October 1962, the USSR upon the orders of its premier Nikita Khrushchev ordered the positioning of Soviet missiles in Cuba, only a short distance from Florida. Though the missiles had not yet been put in place, the missile base was picked up by an American U2 reconnaissance plane. President Kennedy in turn demanded the removal of the missiles and ordered the US Navy to search any boats or ships headed for the island.

This face off came to be known in history as the Cuban Missile Crisis, which went on for several days as Kennedy, Khrushchev and their representatives tried to find a way to defuse the situation. In the end, Khrushchev agreed to remove the missiles from Cuba if the United States would go on record saying that it would not invade Cuba. Likewise, Kennedy gave his nod for the removal of Jupiter missiles from Turkey.

Though a nuclear crisis practically in the backyard of the US had been averted, the threat of Castro remained.

Covertly, the CIA continued with its attempts to assassinate the Cuban leader or at least to topple his regime. Indeed, if Cuban intelligence is to be believed, Castro has apparently been the target of 638 assassination attempts in all. In fact, Castro once reportedly joked that if assassination attempts were an Olympic sport, he would have won a gold medal.

Changing Fortunes

While the resolution of the Cuban Missile Crisis earned both Kennedy and Khrushchev points for restraint, Castro felt humiliated. Not only had the US and USSR kept him completely out of negotiations, but the Organization of American States had been influenced to end diplomatic relations with Cuba.

However, Castro was hardly the kind of personality to remain out of action for long. In the later years of 1960s, he began using his popular political appeal to attack American imperialism and garner support for his philosophy of armed struggle, both in Latin American and African countries. In 1966, Castro founded the Asia-Africa-Latin America People's Solidarity Organization to promote people's revolution on three continents. In 1967, he formed yet another organization, the Latin America Solidarity Organization, which aimed at bringing the fruits of revolution in certain Latin-American countries.

As part of his efforts to gain international recognition, Castro pledged support to Third World countries like Angola, Ethiopia and Yemen mainly in the form of military support. Inevitably, all these initiatives led to huge economic strain on Cuba. Also the disintegration of the Soviet Union meant that Cuba could no longer depend upon cheap sources of oil and a ready market.

Not surprisingly, Castro found ways and means to bring about changes in the economic policy of Cuba, even while keeping his power intact. One of the first signs of change was his visit to United States in 1996 and his appeal to exiled Cubans to return to their homeland and start new businesses. He legalized the US dollar and encouraged tourism to boost foreign spending. As part of the shift in economic policy, Castro ushered in some features of free market economy while also encouraging foreign investment in Cuba.

In 2001, Hurricane Micelle wrought severe damage across the length and breadth of Cuba. Castro however refused humanitarian aid from America and instead agreed to a one-time cash purchase of food from its northern neighbour.

Later Years

It is possible that many of the changes brought about in Castro's policy were the outcome of his advancing years and growing political maturity. Since the late 1990s, there has been constant speculation over the state of Castro's health and his ability to continue to lead the country. In July 2006, Castro went into surgery for gastrointestinal bleeding; at the time, his brother Raul was designated as the temporary leader. Raul was no stranger to politics, having served under Castro's command for decades and in fact already being chosen as Castro's successor. However in 2008, Castro finally gave up the reins of power permanently, letting Raul take over as his successor. The Cuban National Assembly put an official stamp on the succession after it unanimously elected Raul Castro as President of Cuba.

After his retirement from government, Castro took to writing his memoirs and opinions in the form of a column titled, *Reflections of Fidel*. Even now, he remains highly sought after for his views and support on national as well as international political matters. World leaders visiting Cuba continue to seek him out; for instance Iran's Prime Minster, Mahmoud Ahmadinejad met him in 2012, during his visit to Cuba. Again a special meeting was arranged between Castro and Pope Benedict in March 2012, in which the latter sought greater religious freedom for Catholics living in Cuba.

Castro's Legacy

Castro's role in ushering social and economic reforms in Cuba remains undisputed. After the Cuban Revolution, education was made accessible, universal healthcare put in place and land reforms initiated. At the same time though, there were costs in terms of civil liberties. Castro crushed opposition with executions, imprisonment and forced emigration. Indeed his influence crossed the limits of Cuban shores. He was the pivotal figure in the Cuban Missile Crisis which has been described as bringing the planet to the edge of the Third World War. While a dictator exercises absolute power and has the ability to change the history of his nation, seldom does he play such a decisive role in world politics.

□

Idi Amin

D.O.B. – 1925 Country – Uganda
D.O.D. – 16th August, 2003

Idi Amin was a Ugandan military general who led a coup in 1971 against the democratically elected government of Milton Obote and seized absolute power. As a dictator, Idi Amin ruled for eight years, during which Uganda went through several human rights and economic crises. Not only around 300,000 civilians were killed during this period, but the all Indian and Pakistani origin business owners were expelled which in turn broke the back of Ugandan's economy. In 1979, Amin's reign of terror was brought to an end by an uprising led by Ugandan nationalists and supported by the country's exiles as well as help from Tanzanians. The dictator managed to flee the country and lived out the rest of his days in Saudi Arabia.

Early Life

Idi Amin Dada was born in 1925, near Koboko of the West Nile province in Uganda. His father and mother belonged to the Kakwa and Lugbara tribes, respectively. At a very early age, Amin was abandoned by his father and brought up by his mother. Even then he was raised as a member of the Kakwa ethnic group, a small tribe that is native to the region and follows Islam.

There is some confusion as to whether Amin attended a missionary school during his childhood but it is generally accepted by historians that he received a very basic kind of education.

Amin's real training in the world began in 1946 when he joined the King's African Rifles or KAR which was a British colonial regiment composed of African troops. As part of KAR, Amin saw action in many places. In 1949, he was sent to Somalia to suppress the Shifta rebellion and then from 1952 to 1956, he took part in the Mau-Mau expedition during which he fought on the behalf of the British to seize control over the Kenyan rebels.

Military Career

During his years in the KAR, Amin developed a reputation for daring which helped him to rise quickly through the ranks. He became a sergeant major before finally being appointed an 'effendi' – the highest rank bestowed upon an African in the KAR.

At the same time however, Amin was also known for his excessive use of force. More than once, he was ticked off for using extremely brutal methods during military interrogations. As only one of two highest ranking African soldiers in the KAR, Amin was appointed the First Lieutenant of the Ugandan army. He was then sent by his former close colleague Milton Obote to quell cattle stealing in the north of Uganda. However, so brutal were the methods ordered by Amin, that even the colonial British government insisted that he be prosecuted under law. However, instead of reading the writing on the wall, Obote ignored the British demand and instead arranged for Amin to go to the UK to receive further military training.

And yet because of his enthusiasm for dangerous expeditions and his physical vigour – In fact, during his army tenure, Amin became the light heavyweight boxing champion of Uganda and continued to hold the title nine years between 1951 and 1960 – Amin's lapses were ignored by Obote and other Ugandan leaders.

Political Situation

After more than seventy years of colonial rule by the British, in the late 1950s Uganda began to get ready for independence in 1962. The Ugandan People's Congress (UPC) had been at the forefront of the country's struggle for independence and hence its leader Apolo Milton Obote was tipped to form the first independent government. Accordingly, Obote was first made Chief Minister and then succeeded to the office of the Prime Minister of Uganda on October 9, 1962 when Uganda finally got freedom from British rule.

After Amin returned from UK in 1964, Obote promoted him to the rank of a major and gave him the responsibility of controlling the rapidly spreading mutiny in the army. Amin was successful in enforcing discipline and was rewarded with a promotion to the rank of a lieutenant colonel. The two next entered into an alliance in which Amin would lend his support to the Obote government while the latter would give him a free hand in reorganizing the armed forces to Amin's benefit.

This deal however had a covert corrupt objective as well. The two had agreed to join hands to benefit from a smuggling operation in which gold, coffee and ivory would be taken out of Democratic Republic of Congo in exchange of funds and arms that were supposed to reach the troops loyal to the murdered DRC prime minister Patrice Lumumba. However, their leader, General Olenga, complained that despite promising the funds, Obote and Amin never paid the money and this became the basis of a parliamentary investigation carried out on the orders of President Edward Mutebi Mutesa II, also popularly known as 'King Freddie', who was the King of Buganda, a powerful kingdom in south-central Uganda.

The charges against Prime Minister Obote and his military general Idi Amin forced the two to go on a rampage. Obote dissolved the 1960 Constitution of the country, had five rival ministers arrested and declared himself the President of Uganda. At the same time, he also promoted in partner in corruption, Amin, to the rank of a general who consequently became the Chief of Staff. Amin in return, led a military contingent against King Freddie, who was dethroned and forced to flee to Britain in 1966 and where he lead the rest of his life in exile.

Rise to Power

The military success against King Freddie and his influence with Obote only emboldened Amin further. He had already assumed complete control of the Ugandan armed forces and now began to solidify his supremacy, rooting out any opposition by imprisoning and executing any potential rivals. At the same time, Amin ensured that he had a steady source of revenue obtained from smuggling and from supplying arms to rebels in southern Sudan, so that his attempts to garner absolute power could be properly funded.

On the diplomatic front too, Amin seemed to be gaining more influence than Obote. Amin thrashed out deals with British and Israeli agents operating in Uganda according to which in return for strategic or intelligence inputs, his power would be bolstered by foreign help.

All these attempts by Amin at entrenching his own power did not go unnoticed by President Obote. Moreover, two assassination attempts on his life – which though never proved anybody's involvement – brought out Obote's suspicions against Amin out in the open and the President ordered the house arrest of the military general. To restrict the sphere of his influence, Oboto further ensured that Amin was shifted out from the top executive position the army to a less powerful one.

Finally, as Obote left to attend a meeting for a Commonwealth Heads of Government Conference to be held at Singapore, he ordered the arrest of Amin. But taking advantage of Obote's absence in the country, Amin moved swiftly and staged a military coup on January 25, 1971. He declared himself President and the absolute authority in Uganda. He seized control of the entire administration and ordered Obote to stay out of the country. In this way, the recruit who had started out in a colonial army had now become the dictator of the entire country.

Initially, Amin's elevation as the supreme ruler of Uganda was welcomed both at home and abroad. After years of corrupt rule by the Obote government, people were hopeful of a change under Amin. Also many world leaders expected Amin, who had already established ties with Israeli and British agents, would be easier to do business with. Amin recognized the expectations from him and initiated certain symbolic measures that he thought would go down well with his people and even enhance his popularity on the world stage. Thus, he disbanded the dreaded Ugandan Secret Police, which was responsible for wide-scale abuse of power under the Obote regime. Likewise, he ordered the freeing of thousands of political workers who had been imprisoned during the previous government – incidentally, a majority of these freed prisoners Amin's own supporters, a fact that was largely hidden from the world. One of his most popular gestures was to have the body of King Freddie who had died in exile on British soil returned to Uganda for state burial. Though Amin had himself been the one to storm King Freddie's palace and dethrone him, with this initiative he was able to turn the tide of popular opinion on his side.

Years of Misrule

However, the mask of the benevolent dictator did not take long to come off. Though the Uganda Secret Police had been ostensibly disbanded, in its place two different and equally ruthless agencies were put in place. These were the 'State Research Bureau' and 'Public Safety Unit', which eventually carried out for thousands of kidnappings, tortures and executions upon the orders of Amin. They came to have the reputation of 'killer squads' and their primary purpose was to track down and exterminate any kind of opposition to Amin's rule.

The chief source of Amin's fear was the influence still exercised by former Prime Minster of the country and his erstwhile ally, Milton Obote. After having lost power to Amin, Obote fled to Tanzania in 1971. From there, he tried to rally his supporters and with some rebel elements in the Ugandan army – particularly from the Christian-dominated Acholi and Lango ethnic groups – tried to engineer a coup against Amin in 1972. The attempted coup brought out the worst of Amin's brutality. He ordered a purge in the Ugandan armed forces against all personnel of the Acholi and Lango tribes and even carried out bombings in Tanzania in retaliation of the attempted coup being planned from its soil.

Eventually, the witch-hunt against members of the Lango and Acholi tribes expanded to include the civil society as well. People belonging to these ethnic groups or even those from other tribes were picked up at random and subject to the most inhuman interrogation, after which they were usually thrown in jail or more likely, killed. In fact, the Nile Mansions Hotel in Kampala acquired the reputation of a torture cell where tens of thousands of civilians were brought, never to be returned alive.

Despite these many brutal means of exercising control, Amin became increasingly insecure about the loss of power. without any fear of public or international outrage, Amin personally ordered the execution of several high-ranking officials in the country like Anglican Archbishop of Uganda, the chief justice of the country, the chancellor of Makerere College, governor of the Bank of Uganda and many other ministers of his parliament, whom he had perhaps once hand-picked himself. As part of growing paranoia, Amin came to fear even people from his closest political circles; in order to keep the risk of assassinations to a minimum, he is believed to have changed residences on a regular basis.

Economic War

Once the political purge was largely over, Amin next turned his attention to other minority groups of the country, especially those from South Asia. The majority of businesses and industries in Uganda were then owned by people of Indian and to a lesser extent, Pakistani origin. They also formed a sizeable portion of the civil service which ran the day-to-day administration of the country. In order to seize this profitable aspect of economy, Amin raised the bogey of foreign domination and announced that he wanted all businesses to be owned by Ugandans. Thus overnight, at least seventy thousand Asian were told to leave the country – only those who held a British passport were able to emigrate to Britain or elsewhere in the world but even then they had to leave behind their homes and businesses in Uganda. Ostensibly, Amin had done this to nationalize trade and manufacturing in the country but in reality, the businesses abandoned by the Indians were handed over to Amin's own supporters.

Uganda paid a heavy price for such desperate and corrupt practices by Amin. Within a short span of time, the economy of the country headed towards collapse. While Indian-owned businesses and farms had been the mainstay of Ugandan economy, now without a local system in place, commerce, industry and agriculture came to a virtual standstill.

International Relations

In world affairs too, Amin's megalomania and corruption compelled him to take steps that lay squarely against the country's welfare. As an extension of his 'economic war', Amin snapped all diplomatic ties with Britain and nationalized 85 of British-owned businesses. He also broke the erstwhile strategic alliance with Israel and dismissed its military officials from Uganda. Instead Amin now looked to the Soviet Union for international support as well as to the Libyan dictator Muammar Gaddafi for a regional alliance.

However, the biggest international misadventure by Amin was the support given to PLO-led hijackers of an Air France flight in which 256 passengers were taken hostage. On June 27, 1976, the Popular Front for the Liberation of Palestine (PFLP) seized control of an Air France aircraft, that was travelling from Israel to Paris and demanded the release of 53 Palestinian Liberation Organization activists who had been imprisoned by Israel in return for the 256 hostages. Amin not only arranged for a safe place for the hijackers to land at the Entebbe airport but also supplied them with arms and soldiers. However, Israeli commandos launched a covert attack on the Entebbe airport, freeing almost all the hostages.

Amin's reputation was in tatters by the end of the incident. Not only had his support of the terrorists completely isolated Uganda in world affairs but his forces had suffered significant damage too. The air force had suffered particularly heavy losses as its fighter pilots had been destroyed just before the Israeli attack so as to prevent them from supporting the terrorists.

With time, Amin's heightening paranoia had other consequences too. In fact, such was his fear of his own people that he ordered the import of soldiers from Zaire and Sudan. By the time his rule was overthrows in 1972, his army was composed of mainly foreign mercenaries or 'ekebets' and only less than 25% of the soldiers were actually Ugandan.

Later Years

In October 1978, Amin ordered a surprise attack on

a strip of land known as Kagera, located in the northern province of Tanzania and which had a common border with Uganda. The Tanzanian President, Julius Nyerere, retaliated with troops who entered into Uganda, and with the helped of exiled Ugandan forces, captured the Ugandan capital of Kampala.

The last days of Amin were spent as an exile, first in Tanzania and then in Saudi Arabia. On 16 August 2003, Idi Amin Dada died in the Saudi capital city of Jeddah, Arabia of multiple organ failure. Although the Ugandan government announced that his body could be brought back to Uganda and given a state burial here but he was quickly buried in the country of his exile.

His Legacy

To a great extent, Uganda's political and economic disaster was the handiwork of Amin's megalomaniac and foolish efforts.

Some historians suggest that he may have a condition called hypomania which could be responsible for his sporadic emotional outburst as well as moody, intense behavior.

Under him, the Ugandan economy went on a downward spiral and inflation reached an excess of 1,000 percent. Then again there was wide ranging abuse of human rights. In fact, it has been thought that 100,000 to half a million people were imprisoned, tortured and finally killed on his explicit orders or according to covert directions.

□

Sayyad Ali Khameini

D.O.B. – 16th July, 1939 Country – Iran

Sayyad Ali Khameini is the supreme leader of Iran, or 'rahbar', since 1989. As the most powerful religious and political figure in the country, Khameini has ruled with an iron hand ever since he became the President of Iran in 1981. And though he made away for President Rafsanjani in 1989, Khameini had always had his finger firmly on the pulse of the nation.

Early Life

Born as Ali Husseini Khameini on 17 July 1939 to Seyyed Javad Khamenei and Khadijeh Mirdamad, the future leader of Iran was the second eldest of the couple's eight children. Khameini was born in the Iranian town of Mashhad, one of the holiest in the country. Now however he holds the title of Sayyid, which implies that he is directly descended through the patrilineal chain from the holiest leader of Shias, Ali.

Khameini's earliest education was at the hawza of Mashhad where he was taught by religious clerics such as Sheikh Hashem Qazvini and Ayatollah Milani. In 1957, however the young Khameini left for Najaf but the very next year, he left for Mashhad again and then settled in Qom. Here he began his religious studies on an advanced level under the guidance of the most respected Shia scholars of the time, including Ruholla Khomeini who would later become famous for leading the Islamic Revolution and overthrowing the monarchy.

Rise to Power

The influence of Khameini's teachers was evident in his own political choices. He began taking part in the anti-monarchy protests that were gathering steam in Iran from 1963 onwards. Because of his poetical activities, Khameini was imprisoned several times by the country's security services. During the period of Khomeini's exile, Khameini followed his leader's instructions closely and when the former returned to Iran in 1979, Khameini was made part of the extremely powerful Revolutionary Council. After the council was dissolved, Khameini took charge of the ministry of defence in the government and at the same time, was appointed by Ayatollah Khomeini as his personal representative on the Supreme Defence Council.

There were other indications of Khameini's growing influence with the Ayatollah. In 1979 Khomeini gave Khameini the responsibility of leading the Friday prayers in Teheran. This post of the Imam was extremely sought after and in order to succeed to it, Khomeini ordered Hussein-Ali Montazeri – the current Imam – to resign. Other than this, Khameini was made the supervisor of the Islamic Revolutionary Guards for a while. He was also made the representative of the defense commission of the parliament and in the course of this appointment, went to the war front as well.

However, Khameini's growing closeness with Ayatollah Khomeini did not go down well with others. In June 1981, Khameini was the target of an assassination attempt when a bomb, concealed in a tape recorder at a press conference, exploded beside him. Though Khameini escaped death narrowly, he was badly injured and was permanently paralyzed in the right arm.

Rule as President

Another blast later that year led to the death of the secretary-general of the Islamic Republican Party. As a result, Khameini was appointed to fill the vacant position. In 1981, then President of Iran, Mohammad-Ali Rajai, was assassinated after which elections were announced in the country in October. In the national elections, Khameini was voted into power by immense margins and was made the President of Iran. Though initially, Khomeini had earlier ruled that no cleric should head the government, considering Khameini's landslide victory, the Ayatollah modified his policy.

As soon as Khameini had the reins of the government in his hands, he launched a nation-wide crackdown on any kind of political opposition, whether armed or non-violent. Tens of thousands of members of insurgent groups and very often merely those suspected with ties to the political opposition were arrested, tortured and executed. The revolutionary courts became infamous for sending thousands of people to the prison, just on mere suspicion and without having a proper trial. In fact, such was the extent of oppression carried out by the revolutionary courts, that even the government was forced to interfere in 1982, though there was no let down in the hunting down of all opposition group throughout the early decades of the 1980s. Apart from this, Khameini established strong relations with the extremely powerful revolutionary guards, which made his position as President even more secure.

As President of Iran, Khameini played an important role in the shaping of the country's foreign policy. One of his main contributions was leading the country through the Iran-Iraq war of 1980s. During this time, he displayed his leadership with many important strategic decisions and was not even afraid to collide with the injunctions of the Ayatollah too. For instance, Khomeini was of the opinion that after pushing out Iraqi forces from the Iran's territory, their forces should launch a counter-invasion on Iraq, thus hitting out when the enemy was at its weakest. However, Khameini overturned this decision and in it was supported by then Prime Minister of Iran Mir-Hossein Mousavi.

By 1985, Khameini's rule over the government was beyond doubt. Riding high on the success of the Iran-Iraq war as well as having wiped out all forms of political opposition in the country, Khameini proved again victorious in the presidential elections of 1985 and started his second term as the President of Iran.

Spiritual Leadership

Despite Khameini's proximity to Ayatollah Khomeini, the former had never been considered as among the senior most clerics of Iran. In fact, Khameini was accorded with the slightly less important title of *hojatolislam*. But after Khomeini died in 1989, there seemed only one person powerful enough to succeed him to a post which denoted absolute authority in Iran.

Just after the Ayatollah's death, a council of three members was proposed for leadership which would include clerics like Ali Meshkini, Mousavi Ardebili and Khameini. But seeing that no candidate other than Khameini enjoyed wide support, the Assembly of Experts rejected the idea of a Leadership Council and instead elected Khameini as the new Supreme Leader on 4 June 1989 by a majority vote of 60 members out of 74 members present.

However, a problem of the rules presented itself. The Iranian Constitution required that the Supreme Leader should at least be a Marja or a Shia authority who can make legal decisions within the confines of Islamic law for followers. Since Khameini was at that time not yet a Marja, he was made the temporary Supreme Leader and eventually the constitution was amended to make Khameini's ascension possible. On 6 August 1989, the Assembly of Experts met again and this time confirmed the appointment of Khameini as the Supreme Leader of Iran with an overwhelming majority of 60 votes out of 64 present.

Once he was made the Supreme Leader or rahbar, Khameini became the absolute authority in the country. In a series of lectures, Ayatollah Ruhollah Khomeini had laid down that in Iran, the top ruler should be an Islamic jurist serving as "guardian". This all-powerful guardian would be called rahbar by the Iranian Constitution and all political decisions would have to be approved by this leader if it was to be lawful and applicable to the country. This effectively meant that the 'rahbar' held complete power in his hands since even a democratically elected president would first have to seek the approval of the supreme leader before he could take charge of his office.

Continuing Influence

By and large, Khameini had been able to portray a picture of distance from the day-to-day affairs of the government. He rarely gave press conferences or interviews and appears only on special events like the Friday prayers or on anniversaries of nationally important days. This proved useful for perpetuating his image of the leader as more of a 'guide', rather than the executive arm of the government.

During the early 1990s, Khameini had a good relationship with then President of the country, Hashemi Rafsanjani. However, in 1997 Mohammad Khatami came to power who had more of a reformist agenda and this set up a friction with Khameini. Khatami could only remain in power till 2005 after which Khameini personally took an interest in the presidential candidates.

Khameini's choice fell upon Mahmoud Ahmadinejad who had been mayor of Tehran but was relatively inexperienced in politics. However, Ahmadinejad was a conservative unlike his predecessor Khatami. Though Khameini ostensibly projected an image of neutrality in the presidential elections, he made some speeches in which an indirect support for the candidature of Ahmadinejad was evident. Also the overwhelming victory of a political newcomer like Ahmadinejad in the presidential elections of 2005 proved that some sort of validation from Khameini had been present.

However, to preserve a picture of neutrality, Khameini on some occasions spoke out against the policies of Ahmadinejad, leading many political observers to speculate about whether the president had fallen from the Ayatollah's favour.

These speculations found further currency in the presidential elections of 2009. Ahmadinejad found himself challenged by several presidential candidates, none of who could have made it this far without the approval of the Council of Guardians. This was a body of jurists that was responsible for supervising elections and reviewing legislation. Half of the members of the Council of Guardians were directly chosen by Khameini and it was inconceivable that he was not aware or approve of the challengers to Ahmadinejad.

One of the more influential presidential candidates for the 2009 elections was former Mir Hossein Mousavi who had served as the prime minister of Iran from 1981 to 1989. Reformist political groups of different kinds rallied around Mousavi, alleging their support for his presidential campaign. Buoyed by this kind of following, Mousavi turned out to be a formidable opponent to Ahamdinejad and pre-election polls predicted that the national elections would be a close fight.

However, soon after the end of the polls, Ahmadinejad was declared to have garnered more than 60 percent of the votes, and with this absolute majority was thus declared the clear victor of the presidential race. Khameini too endorsed the results and the path for Ahmadinejad for another presidential term seemed clear.

But Mousavi was in no mood to relent. He rallied the opposition behind him, charging that the polls had been unfair and therefore the results were not legitimate. Soon enough protests broke out in Teheran and at other places in the country where supporters of the opposition put up massive roadblocks and carried out huge demonstrations.

Sensing the popular discontent, Khameini stepped in and ordered the council of Guardians to carry out an official inquiry into the charges of election irregularities posed by the opposition. The Council responded by announcing that the election results would go through a partial recount. However, the opposition vehemently rejected this proposal and declared that nothing short of an annulment of the election results would be acceptable to them.

Soon Teheran and other cities were rocked by protests and the state of massive discontent continued for around a week. The state of affairs compelled Khameini to break his silence – he once again confirmed the victory of Ahmadinejad and warned that henceforth anyone who would oppose the election result would be dealt with great severity. This effectively put a stop to any further protests by the opposition and compelled the nation to accept Ahmadinejad as their president for another term.

Other Policies

In recent times, Khameini has shown an interest in the economic liberalization of Iran's economy. In 2007, he ordered the government officials to put the country's privatization policy on fast track. In 2004, under Khameini, Article 44 of the constitution had already been over-ruled which claimed that the core infrastructure of Iran would remain under state control. As part of economic liberalization, Khameini also ordered the Justice Ministry to set up courts which would protect ownership rights of businesses and asset. This in turn would encourage private investment in the country and assure investors of the security of their businesses.

Yet another important aspect of Khameini's reign had been Iran's policy on nuclear energy. In fact, Iran's nuclear program continues to be a subject of intense international debate. Khameini had always insisted that Iran is looking to develop nuclear technology for civilian purposes because of the limited reserves of oil and natural gas reserves. However, in recent times then Khameini also issued a fatwa saying that Islam actually forbids the production, stockpiling and use of nuclear weapons and reiterating that Iran's nuclear program is only compelled by energy requirements.

Legacy

Though Khameini has distanced himself from the regular affairs of the government, by a series of checks and balances. He ensures that there is no loosening of his grip on absolute power in Iran. Most importantly he ensures his control over the Revolutionary Guard and it is this force that keeps him in power.

Also there has been some change in his perception of the West, especially the United States. While in the past, his discourse has always painted US as the 'Monstrous Other', intent only on overturning the Islamic Revolution in Iran, recently Khameini's speeches have displayed a more nuanced conception of the America as a complex social reality, one which is fighting its own demons like economic crises and violent military engagements in different parts of the world. Even then despite some changes in perceptions, Khameini seems unlikely to change his anti-American stance anytime soon – though what can be hoped for is gradual widening of democracy in Iran so that he can better legitimize his authority in Iran before the sight of the world.

And though Iran's youth seems uninterested in who will replace him as the Ayatollah or the Supreme Leader, Khameini does not seem to be willing to let go of his authority just yet. In recent years, there has been some speculation about the state of his health. But he has ensured and carefully orchestrated public appearances and charged anti-national agencies of trying to demoralize the nation by raising suspicions about the Ayatollah's health. Today Khameini has been a cleric for sixty years, and at the leader of a religious revolution for more than twenty. His power over the government of Iran though not always visible, remains complete.

□

Mengitsu Haile Mariam

D.O.B. – 21st May, 1937 Country – Ethiopia

Beginning his career as a private in the Ethiopian army, Mengitsu Haile Mariam rose to the position of the chairman of the ruling military government which deposed Emperor Haile Selassie in 1974 and established a quasi-socialist government in Ethiopia. Within the next decade, Mengitsu reorganized the structure of the ruling party of the country in a way which made him the head of the state and the absolute authority in Ethiopia. However, this rise to power was marked by widespread abuse of power and mass killings. Towards the end of 1980s, however he began to lose control of the government and 1991 he was forced to resign. Mengitsu fled to Zimbabwe and continues to live in exile there even after being convicted in absentia by an Ethiopian court of genocide.

Early Life

Little is definitively known about the early life of Mengitsu Haile Mariam other than the fact that he was born on born on 21 May 1937 in Addis Ababa. When Mengitsu was just an eight year old boy, his mother died in childbirth and along with his two other siblings, he was sent to live with his grandmother. After a few years, he came back to live with his father Hailemariam Wolde Ayana but could never settle down to full-fledged family life.

Instead Mengitsu left to join the army at a very young age and enlisted as a private. However, being an enterprising lad, he caught the attention of Eritrean-born general Aman Andom, who promoted him to the rank of a sergeant and then motivated him to enroll at the Holeta Military Academy. After passing out from the Academy, Mengitsu was taken under the wings of General Aman, who when posted to Third Division of the Ethiopian army ensured Mengitsu accompanied him to Harar and got him posted as the Ordnance officer in the Third Division.

Soon however Mengitsu got into a conflict with the current Third Division Commander General Haile Baykedagn and it was only by his proximity to General Aman that allowed him to leave for six months' training in Maryland, USA. These incidents of his early career would leave a lasting impact on Mengitsu as he later he would extract revenge against General Haile Baykedagn and develop a deep hatred of Americans for having suffered racial discrimination during his training in the US.

After his return from the US, though Mengitsu focused on advancing his career. By 1974, he had risen to the rank of major. His undoubted leadership qualities made him popular among his fellow junior officers and earned him the loyalty of other ranks in the Third Division.

Rise to Power

While Mariam was climbing up the military ladder, Ethiopia was going through a political churning. The country had been under the rule of Emperor Haille Selassie since 1916 but the monarchy had little to show for it. Instead the country was riddled with poverty and corruption. Absentee landlords based in the northern part of the country imposed heavy taxes on peasant farmers in the rural south and west whose lands had been conquered by northern armies a generation earlier. So when a wave of famines hit Ethiopia and the oil crisis of 1973 further depleted the economy, long simmering discontent of the people burst forth and a series of rebellions began taking place in the country. Seizing this opportunity, the military establishment deposed the king in 1974, which came to be known as the Ethiopian Revolution.

After the fall of the Imperial government, the military took control and established Provisional Military Advisory Council (PMAC), or Derg which was made up of 126 members. In July 1974, the PMAC elected Mengistu as its chairman and later in September, when the PMAC was formally organized, Mengitsu was appointed first vice-chairman of the council, a position he continued to hold until he took complete control in February 1977. However, the change in regime and Mengitsu's own rise to power was not without violence – in November 1974, around 60 members of the Haile Selassie government were executed, thus anticipating in a way, Mengitsu's complete intolerance and use of brutality in dealing with opposition of any kind.

Led by Mengitsu, the military government of Ethiopia initiated several economic and social reforms along a socialist model. Among the earliest of these was a major land reform in 1975, in which smaller farms were taken over by the administration and collectivized. Also foreign-owned banks were nationalized just as factories and insurance companies were brought under domestic or direct state control.

Mengitsu's growing power in the military government as well as a series of socialist reforms did not go down too well with the older officers of the military, who had ties to the traditional social and economic elite of the country. But Mengitsu, with a combination of ruthless repression as well as populist reform ensured that his influence both within the government and amidst the people continued to widen. Thus, in 1976, he was promoted to the rank of lieutenant colonel and just the next year, he became the commander-in-chief of the entire Ethiopian armed forces. Mengitsu's authority in the military government was now complete.

The Red Terror

Though Mengitsu had established his supremacy in the military government, he still faced challenges from the civil society. Despite some reform measures, the economy was still struggling and several social injustices continued. To add to these, news of corruption in the military government incensed the civil populace, who were already suffering from economic hardships. Consequently, between 1977 and 1978, Ethiopia witnessed a series of uprisings led by younger, politically radical sect of the population. Bureaucrats who had lost power with the arrival of the military government in Ethiopia also joined the protests.

Despite growing unrest, Mengitsu was in no mood to listen to the people's grievances. He ordered the military government to crush the uprisings with an iron hand. In the resulting state-sponsored violence that came to be known as the 'Red Terror', thousands of young Ethiopians as well as members of civil society were brutally silenced by the military police and the insurgency stamped out.

Alignment with Soviet Bloc

No sooner than Mengitsu had dealt with domestic turbulence than Ethiopia became the victim of external aggression as well. In 1977, Somalia sent its forces to invade the eastern border of Ethiopia. Though the invasion was a threat to the security of Ethiopia, it also gave Mengitsu to further solidify and finally legitimize his supremacy in the government. When the United States refused to offer any military assistance to Ethiopia, Mengitsu turned to the Soviet Union for help. The latter provided the Ethiopian government not only arms and ammunition to beat back the invading Somali forces but also military advice and diplomatic support on the international stage. By the end of the 1970s, Mengistu had ensured that Ethiopia had the second largest army in the entire sub-Saharan Africa, as well as a powerful navy and air force.

The military alliance with USSR soon paved the way for ideological and economic association as well. Under Mengitsu, the military government of Ethiopia aggressively embarked on a version of Leninist and Marxist economic measures. Taking off from the earlier reforms, all industry and business – whether foreign-owned or privately-held – was brought under state control. Moreover, any undeveloped urban property and rental property was taken over by the government. Rural land was nationalized so that the system of collective farming could be developed. In the process, the biggest traditional landowners of the country like the Ethiopian Church, the royal family as well as members of the erstwhile nobility had to cede their huge estates. Farmer, who had earlier suffered at the hands of absentee landlords were now facing a different problem – forced labour on collective farms. Also the government decreed that all agricultural products would be controlled and distributed by the government, thus doing away with the free market system.

Ostensibly, the reforms were pushed to stop the concentration of wealth in a few hands and redistribute it among the poor. But in reality, these measures were riddled with corruption and inefficiency. Though nationalized, farms and companies were often placed under control of those close to Mengitsu or his cronies. Also without a network of experienced and skilled human resource framework to fall back upon, the expulsion of foreign owners and employees in industries and business spelled doom for the economy. Also Ethiopia continued to reel under droughts and the famine of 1984 especially brought large scale suffering for its people which was compounded by corruption and misguided economic policies.

Formation of New Government

During the mid-1980s, Mengistu replaced the PMAC with a new ruling body, the COPWE or the committee to form the party of the workers of Ethiopian central committee of COPWE comprised of seven top leaders, who were chosen from PMAC's own central committee. Mengitsu was appointed the head of this new ruling body of the government – chairman of both the executive and central committees of COPWE. Finally, in September 1984, as part of the celebrations of the tenth anniversary of the Ethiopian revolution, party of the workers of Ethiopia was formally brought into existence and Mengitsu announced himself as not only head of the party and commander-in-chief of the armed forces but also as chairman of the PMAC, head of the supreme planning council as well as that of the council of ministers. With this, Mengitsu now possessed all authority in Ethiopia and emerged as the absolute ruler of the country.

Along with establishing himself as the dictator of Ethiopia, Mengitsu also took charge of the foreign policy of the country. Because of his aggressive socialist reforms, he came to be seen as the true revolutionary leader of Africa – something of a Fidel Castro figure of the continent. In order to cement Ethiopia's alliance with the Eastern bloc, Mengitsu between the years 1977 to 1984 made seven visits to the former Soviet Union, besides extending diplomatic relations with other anti-US countries like Libya, Cuba, Mozambique and South Yemen. In 1982, Ethiopia hosted the meetings of Organization of African Unity and in recognition of his commitment, Mengitsu was appointed the OAU head from 1983 to 1984.

Though Mengitsu had put in place a new ruling body in 1984, all the fanfare could not prevent Ethiopia from the effects of a devastating drought the same year. Ethiopia was always an agricultural economy and thus especially vulnerable to natural calamities but this time the consequences were even more disastrous. As a result of the forced collectivization of farms and the relocation of entire populations, the country could not withstand the impact of the drought and the resulting famine brought people on the brink of starvation.

Not surprisingly, uprisings against the government started breaking out in different places of the country. To add to this, there were armed rebellions in the northern regions of Tigray and Eritrea and by September 1987, it was clear that the government was under attack. Mengitsu and his leaders however used the most brutal repressive measures to control the uprisings – thousands of supporters of rebel groups were arrested, tortured and killed without any recourse to law or trial. Despite unleashing a wave of fear and violence, Mengitsu started losing ground and when the Soviet Union withdrew support in 1991, he was forced to step down. After resigning from his post, Mengitsu fled to Zimbabwe in order to avoid arrest and imprisonment or even possible execution by his rivals.

Current Status

Later governments that came to power in Ethiopia tried to extradite Mengitsu from Zimbabwe so that the former dictator could stand trial in his country on charges of genocide. In December 2000, Mengitsu was found guilty of the crime of genocide and next year, sentenced to life imprisonment after an Ethiopian court tried him in absentia. In fact, the sentence was commuted to death in May 2008 after the prosecution successfully appealed in the Ethiopian High Court that the extent and nature of Mengitsu's crimes merited a far more severe punishment.

As of now though, Mengitsu remains in Zimbabwe and all efforts to extradite him to Ethiopia have failed.

□

Saddam Hussein

D.O.B. – 28th April, 1937 Country – Iraq
D.O.D. – 30th Dec., 2006

One of the most prominent leaders of the Middle East in twentieth century, Saddam Hussein was the President of Iraq for over two decades. During this time, he established a dictatorial regime which despite having brought about some benefits of secularism and progress, left behind a legacy of political repression, human rights abuses and international conflict from which the nation has yet to emerge fully.

Early Life

Born as Saddam Hussein Abd al-Majid al-Tikriti, on April 28, 1937, in Tikrit, the future dictator of Iraq had a difficult childhood. One tragedy after another assailed his family around the time of his birth – a few months before Saddam was born, his father left the family and some later Saddam's older brother succumbed to cancer. Suffering from depression, Saddam's mother was unable to care for the child. Then aged only three, Saddam was thus sent to Baghdad to live with his uncle, Khairallah Talfah. Though Saddam's mother remarried and called back the child, an abusive step-father once again compelled Saddam to seek out his uncles' guardianship and he continued to stay in Baghdad.

Saddam was thus largely raised by his uncle Khairallah Talfah through his childhood. Talfah was an orthodox Sunni Muslim and a firm opponent of British colonial presence. He was an ardent supporter of Arab nationalism which believed the re-unification of all Arab states in the Middle East under a common spiritual and political leadership. These views had a considerable influence on the growing boy and in future would go on to play a deciding role in Saddam's political career.

Saddam received his education in Baghdad. Initially, he attended the nationalistic al-Karh Secondary School in Baghdad and then enrolled in a law school but left after three years without graduating. In 1957, when Saddam was 20, he became a member of the Ba'ath Party, which was strongly based on the ideology of pan-Arab nationalism. Saddam, under his uncle's influence, was already in favour of the unity of Arab states in the Middle East and hence he started working diligently for the political objectives of the Ba'ath Party.

The very next year that Saddam joined the Ba'ath Party a military coup led by General Abd al-Karim Qasim overthrew the king of Iraq Faisal II in what came to be known as the 14 July Revolution. Qasim now became President of the country. The nationalists of Iraq had high expectations from President Qasim, who however turned out an opponent of the newly-formed United Arab Republic. Also Qasim was suspicious of communist political groups and both these reasons put him firmly in conflict with the Ba'ath Party. Saddam and some other Ba'ath activists next planned an assassination of Qasim in which, the President was shot several times but survived in the end. Saddam too received a bullet in his leg, though the President's driver was killed in the assassination attempt. While Saddam managed to escape to Syria several of his co-conspirators were arrested, convicted and executed.

Saddam stayed only for a short while at Syria which was actually the originating state of the Ba'athist ideology. From here he went to Egypt where he attended law school and stayed till 1963.

In the same year, President Qasim's government was toppled during a coup which came to be known as the Ramadan Revolution of 1963. Under the new dispensation, leaders of the Ba'ath Party were appointed to the cabinet, which was headed by Abdul Salam Arif as President. It was suspected that United States and United Kingdom were also involved in the deposition of former President Qasim and in the establishment of the Ba'ath government. However, because of infighting within the top leaders of the Ba'ath Party, President Arif dismissed and arrested certain members of his own government in what was later known as the November 1963 Iraqi coup détat. Around this time, Saddam – who had returned from Egypt following the downfall of Qasim's government – also found himself on the wrong side of prison bars.

Despite being jailed, Saddam continued to be actively involved in the political events of the time. And eventually his resourcefulness paid off. He was made deputy secretary of the Regional Command in 1966. Not long after, Saddam was able to flee from prison and over the following years, began building his political support base among other Ba'ath activists and sympathizers.

Rise to Power

In 1968, the Ba'ath Party engineered another coup – this time replacing the weak Abdul Rahman Arif with top Ba'ath leader Ahmed Hassan al-Bakr as the President. In this bloodless coup, Saddam played an important role since he along with Salah Omar al-Ali motivated the Ba'ath supporters in the military forces to bring about the change in regime. For his contribution in the successful coup, Saddam was made al-Bakr's deputy in the government as well as appointed the deputy chairman of the Ba'athist Revolutionary Command Council.

Though Saddam had now attained power and was the second most powerful official in the state, he had not forgotten how party infighting could destabilize the government. As a result, he took several harsh measures in wiping out political opposition and ensuring that his position remained secure. This was among the first indications of his ruthless ways which later emerged as full-fledged dictatorship.

Though al-Bakr was more senior to Saddam and better respected in the Ba'ath Party, the latter introduced a series of measures which would accumulate power in his own hands. One of his earliest intentions was to bring about stability in government as well as political structure of the country. For centuries, Iraq had been riddled with factionalism along religious, tribal and economic lines. There were political groups and splinter groups within them which were constantly fighting amongst themselves. This had not only led to myriad coups and depositions but had also weakened the economy of the country and demoralized the people.

Saddam realized that if he was to enjoy power, he would have to rein in the bickering political groups in the country. He took measures to create an iron-tight security system that would prevent coups within the power structure and insurrections from outside. This security apparatus was composed of Ba'athist paramilitary groups as well as the People's Army so as to prevent top officials of either one from getting too powerful. However, these forces often worked in extra-constitutional ways, employing methods like torture, coercion and assassination to meet its ends. Saddam ordered the launch of Iraq's first chemical weapons program. Also he personally supervised the working of the secret police or Mukhbarat which not only reported on any nascent political opposition in the country but controlled the civil society by embedding government sympathizers as newspaper editors, journalists and artists in the media as well as other civil organizations of the country.

Reforms

Though Saddam followed a policy of zero-tolerance to political opposition, he also knew that in order to build a wide support base in the country, he would have to address some of the people's concerns. With this is mind, he initiated reforms in varied aspects of the economy – agriculture, industry and infrastructure – as well as in society.

One of the earliest social reforms was in the field of education. The government drive to universal free schooling up to the highest education levels was spear-headed by two main programmes – "the National Campaign for the Eradication of Illiteracy" and the campaign for "Compulsory Free Education in Iraq," which Saddam personally headed. As a result of these campaigns within shortest possible period, millions of households became literate in Iraq. Also under Saddam, the country now boasted one of the most developed public health structures in the Middle East for which Saddam received a UNESCO award too. Apart from free universal education and free hospital treatment, Saddam's government undertook other welfare measures like providing support to families of soldiers who had been martyred or injured in the line of duty. Because of all these social reforms, within a few years, Iraq could boast of one of the highest human development standards in the Middle East.

Saddam also realized that without strengthening the economy, all kinds of social reforms would be meaningless. As a result, he introduced the policy of offering subsidies to farmers. With an eye to appeasing Ba'athist supporters in the rural regions of Iraq, Saddam expedited the mechanization of agriculture and also distributed farms to landless peasants. Workers of the Ba'ath Party established farm cooperatives; in 1974-75, the government raised the budget for agricultural development to twice the existing amount. In fact, farming subsidies were fixed at such high levels that were unheard of in other Arab countries of the region.

However at the centre of Saddam's economic reforms was the oil industry. On 1 June 1972, he nationalized the oil-fields of Iraq thus putting an end to international influence in this sector which till now, had been the norm in Iraq. This was a highly astute move because as the energy crisis hit the global economy next year, Iraq was in a position to benefit from huge revenues which not only helped Saddam to fuel the domestic economy but strengthen his power in the government and popularity amidst the people.

At the same time Saddam recognized that for the economy to be stable, it could not depend just on oil reserves. Consequently, he directed the diversification of the economy which was financed by the largesse that had been accumulated after the 1973 energy crisis. Primary on the agenda of the diversification drive was a national infrastructure campaign which oversaw the building of highways, roads, airports, rail network and commercial ports. This not only paid dividends to the economy but further reaped popular support for Saddam. Likewise, he ordered the development of industries and mining activities other than directly connected with the energy sector. As a result of such measures, Iraq saw rapid electrification of its cities, towns and villages even. Whereas the Iraqi economy had largely been agricultural in the pre-Saddam years, with him formulating economic policies, the country was rapidly industrialized and the urban populace increased substantially.

President of Iraq

Once Saddam had established his influence within the government and outside amidst the people, it was only a matter of time before he went for the top position in the country. This opportunity presented itself in 1979, when the current President al-Bakr began talks of unification of Iraq and Syria. Saddam realized that such a measure would sideline him in the government and he forced al-Bakr to resign. On July 16, 1979, Saddam Hussein declared himself President of Iraq and just a week later, he had 68 of Ba'ath Party leaders arrested and convicted of treason while 22 of them were even sentenced to death. By early August 1979, the political purge ordered by Saddam saw hundreds of his opponents executed and any source of protest effectively extinguished. With this swift ruthless move, Saddam made it evident to everyone in the country that he and only he had absolute power.

Iran-Iraq War

When in 1979, Ayatollah Khomeini led the Islamic Revolution in Iran, Saddam got worried that a similar uprising in Iraq might destabilize his power which partly rested on the support of the Sunni-minority in Iraq. Thus, in 1980, Saddam ordered his forces to invade the southern border of Iran, Khuzestan, which was rich in oil reserves. Though Saddam was clearly the aggressor, most world powers threw their weight behind the Iraqi dictator for fear of the spread of Islamic radicalism from Khomeini's Iran into the rest of the region. The timidity of the Western powers only heightened Saddam's willfulness and he showed no qualms in using chemical weapons, threatening nuclear warfare and killing millions of Kurdish people. After eight long years, when the war had taken many thousand lives on both sides, the leaders of the two countries finally agreed on a ceasefire.

However, Saddam's thirst for territorial aggression was still not appeased. Also years of war had created havoc with Iraq's resources and thus he looked towards Kuwait to make good his losses. Using the justification that historically Kuwait was part of Iraq, Saddam ordered his troops to invade the country on August 2, 1990. This time however international reaction was quick and strong. When Saddam continued to ignore a deadline set by the UN Security Council for withdrawal of Iraqi troops, then the US together with other Western forces launched a counterattack and within just six weeks had driven out the Iraqi forces from Kuwait.

Saddam's irresponsible foreign policy had brought war and suffering on its people. No wonder then various rebel groups – especially those led by Shiite and Kurdish people – started organizing uprising against the dictator in the country. Saddam responded to these rebellions with brutal force and instead of resolving the legitimate demands of people, his security forces arrested and executed thousands of rebel supporters.

Saddam's government was increasingly being weakened by international forces too. Iraq was already under economic sanctions and now Saddam's repeated violation of no-fly air spaces resulted in Allied Forces bombing large parts of the country.

In the aftermath of World Trade Centre bombing, the US in combination with other Western powers launched a massive military operation against Iraq on grounds that Saddam was stockpiling weapons of mass destruction. Within just a few weeks, Iraq's government and military had been deposed and on April 9, 2003, the Allied Powers seized the control of Baghdad. Saddam, incredibly, managed to escape. Over the next few months, Saddam continued to release audio and video recordings from his hiding place, rallying his supporters to organize a resistance against US-led forces. Finally on December 13, 2003, Saddam was captured from a small underground bunker near a farmhouse near Tikrit and transferred to an American prison in Baghdad. Eventually on June 30, 2004, he was formally handed over to the interim Iraqi government so that he could be tried for crimes against humanity.

Even during the trial, Saddam remained completely defiant – he questioned the court's authority to try him and vehemently denied all the charges of murder, torture and genocide leveled against him. On November 5, 2006, the court found Saddam guilty of crimes against humanity and sentenced him to death. Though the sentence was appealed, later it was upheld even by the Court of Appeals. Finally on December 30, 2006, at Camp Justice, an Iraqi base in Baghdad, Saddam was hanged to death. He was buried the next day in Al-Awja, his place of birth.

His Legacy

Though Saddam Hussein turned out to be one of the best known leaders of the Middle East, he left behind a mixed legacy. He did a lot to transform Iraq from the almost medieval, agrarian economy to a highly developed, urbanized and industrialized country. The social reforms that he introduced ensured that, during the late 1970s at least, Iraq could claim to be true welfare state – a rare feat among the Middle Eastern countries.

However all the initial reforms were later nullified by the intensely despotic policies followed by Saddam. He demolished all political opposition by intensely repressive measures and ordered the deaths of millions of Kurds and Shiites in his country. Finally by subjecting Iraq to repeated wars, first against Iran which went on for eight long years and then against Kuwait which earned the full wrath of western military might, Saddam ruined his country and brought untold misery to its people. All this tangled up the geopolitical dynamics of the region in such a way that even now Iraq has not been able to fully emerge from the shadows of suffering and violence.

□

Muammar Al Gaddafi

D.O.B. – 7th June, 1942
D.O.D. – 20th Oct., 2011

Country – Libiya

Muammar Al Gaddafi was the ruler of Libya for over four decades. From 1969, when he successfully led a coup against then King Idris I to 2011 when he was ousted by a popular revolution. During the years, he was in power in Syria, he brought about some reforms but often at the cost of repression and all the excesses that come with dictatorship. Internationally, Gaddafi acquired the reputation of an eccentric leader who nevertheless ruled Syria with an iron hand and often went against majority world opinion.

Early Life

Born in a tent at a desert outpost in Surt, Libya, Gaddafi was the son of an itinerant Bedouin farmer. Since at the time Bedouins kept no birth records, Gaddafi's year of birth is speculated to be 1942 or early 1943.

He was supposed to be a good student at the secondary school that he attended in Sabha, a market town that was relatively more developed than his birthplace. It was here that he first became interested in politics. As he was growing up, many significant events were taking place in Middle East, like the 1948 Arab-Israeli War, the 1952 Revolution in Egypt, the 956 Suez Crisis as well as formation of the United Arab Republic, which however was in existence only between 1958 and 1961. One of the figures in Arab politics who captured Gaddafi's imagination was the Egyptian President, Gamal Abdel Nasser. Gaddafi was greatly impressed by the political changes implemented by Nasser in the Arab Republic of Egypt as well as the ideology of pan-Arab nationalism. Apart from this, Gaddafi agreed with his political idol on the latter's stand against Western colonialism, Zionism and any other form of neo-colonialism an instead rooted for a movement from capitalism to socialism.

Political Context of Syria

During the time of Gaddafi's childhood, Libya was largely treated as a spoil of war among the Western powers. Italy had occupied it in early 1940s as part of the Second World War but had been forced to engage with British forces intent on restricting the influence of Axis countries. All this led to Libya to be embroiled in the North African Campaign of the Second World War. After the end of the war, Libya found itself at the centre of British-French conflict, each of which wanted to control the country. Eventually, the United Nations deemed that Libya be granted political independence. Accordingly in 1951, the United Kingdom of Libya was created by the UN which placed the country under the rule of a monarch, Idris I. Though supposed to be pro-Western, the king turned out to be anti-democratic in his policies. He banned all political parties and put in place an absolute monarchy, thus replacing the UN-mandated federal structure with a highly centralized governing system. Moreover, the system of royal patronage was rife in the kingdom which led to extreme corruption as well as wide regional and economic disparity.

All these events had a significant influence on the young Gaddafi. Early on he took a strong stand against Western colonialism and interference by such countries which eventually hardened into an anti-American and anti-NATO ideology during the years of his rule.

Rise to Power

After leaving school, Gaddafi joined the Royal Military Academy at Benghazi. While in the military, he founded a secret rebel group in 1964 named, the Central Committee of the Free Officers Movement. Around this time, he also travelled around Libya seeking information of other rebel groups ready to rise against the monarchy and scouting for sympathizers. Incredibly, the government's intelligence mechanism did not see him as a threat and ignored his potentially subversive activities.

In April 1966, Gaddafi left for England for a military training course. Though initially he did well in the course, after a while he found it difficult to adjust to the foreign culture, its people and in protest went about wearing Libyan robes while roaming at Piccadilly in London. This was one of the first instances when Gaddafi would assert his Arab identity, especially in an eccentric manner.

By the end of 1960s, popular revolts had already started breaking out against the misrule of King Idris I in Libya. But when Egypt lost to Israel in the 1968 Six Days War, supporters of Arab nationalism vented their anger against King Idris who was seen as pro-Western, pro-Israel and hence anti-Arab.

When in mid-1969, King Idris along with his family left the country for his Mediterranean summer vacation, the Central Committee of the Free Officers Movement led by Gaddafi decided to take advantage of the vacuum in leadership. In a swift, bloodless coup on 1 September 1969, Gaddafi and his supporters ousted the Crown Prince Sayyid Hasan ar-Rida al-Mahdi as-Sanussi, defeated the monarchists and seized power after which Gaddafi renamed the country as Libyan Arab Republic.

Political Reorganization

The government of the new republic was made up of twelve members of the central committee of the Free Officers who had declared themselves as the Revolutionary Command Council. Gaddafi set himself up as the Chairman of the RCC and in the process, became the *de facto* head of state. He had already taken the rank of a colonel and now he appointed himself as the commander-in-chief of the Libyan armed forces. Though ostensibly the twelve-member RCC was supposed to take major decisions of the government, in reality it was Gaddafi whose word was law.

After having seized power, the RCC led by Gaddafi was eager to consolidate its authority. To this end, Gaddafi ordered a purge in the political and armed forces which involved the identification and imprisonment of all monarchists as well as members of the Senussi clan to which King Idris belonged. People's Courts were set up to try politicians and journalists who were either related to the monarchists or at least sympathetic to them. This was just the beginning of long spell of political repression that would be practiced in Gaddafi's regime and in these early days, all trade unions were banned in May 1970, while a couple of years later in 1972, the workers even lost their right to strike or publish their own newspapers.

Seeking to promote a pan-Libyan identity, Gaddafi next turned his attention to the tribal leaders who mostly commanded the allegiance of specific ethnic groups. When the tribal leaders refused to give up their traditional authority, the Gaddafi-led RCC tried to denounce them as continuation of the ideology of the earlier government. In fact, in August 1971, a Sabha military court tried many of these tribal leaders on charges of counter-revolutionary activities which heightened tension between the traditional leaders and the new government. In order to restrict the influence of tribal leaders, Gaddafi floated the Arab Socialist Union (ASU) whose main purpose was to hype up the anti-monarchist revolutionary sentiment across the country. More importantly for Gaddafi's purpose the ASU recognized the RCC as its "Supreme Leading Authority" which in turn meant that his control over all political activity was assured.

Economic Measures

However, Gaddafi was astute enough to accompany this political repression with some economic reforms for the country. And in a country like Libya, this had to revolve around its main export, crude oil. As soon as Gaddafi came to power, he declared in October 1969 that the present terms of oil trade were starkly skewed against Libya and in favour of Western energy giants. In December the same year, Libya raised the price of its crude oil, thus paving the way for other OPEC countries to follow suit. This resulted in an increase in the global price of oil and compelled the energy multinational companies to thrash a deal with the Libyan regime. Known as the Tripoli Agreement, his resulted in the oil companies granting income tax, back-payments and higher prices to Libya which roughly earned additional revenues of $1 billion in just the first year of its rule.

However, Gaddafi was not to be satisfied with mere economic gains and he aimed for political as well as diplomatic ones too. Thus, in 1971, he launched a nationalization rive according to which the British Petroleum's share of the British Petroleum-N.B. Hunt Sahir Field was taken over by the Libyan government. The most important step in nationalization came in September 1973, when all foreign oil-producing companies working out of Libya were declared to be nationalized. Though this step was inspired by socialism, for Gaddafi this turned out to be an effective way of garnering popular approval as well. For one, it led to a manifold rise in gross domestic product which shot up from $3.8 billion in 1969 to $13.7 billion in 1974, and a staggering $24.5 billion in 1979 also the revenues earned by nationalization to some extent was allowed to percolate down to the population as a result of which the average per capita income improved from $40 in 1951 to $8,170 in 1979, thus leaving even some Western economies like Italy behind.

Social Reforms

Along with economic measures, Gaddafi also introduced some social reforms. As part of this, compulsory education was expanded from six years to nine years and university education was made free. At the same time, the RCC launched adult literacy programs which went a great way in raising the literacy levels of the country. New institutions of higher learning like Beida University were set up while older ones like Benghazi University and Tripoli University were developed.

All such measures were funded by the revenues earned from higher prices that the RCC had set for Libyan oil as well as from nationalization of Libyan oil interests. Many other welfare policies were initiated like improved healthcare as well as house-building projects. One beneficial consequence of these policies was that the public sector got a strong boost which in turn raised the employment rate in the country.

Pan-Arab Nationalism

Despite undertaking many social and economic reforms, Gaddafi was careful to emphasize his Arab identity. He saw himself as the successor of the anti-Italian fighter Omar Mukhtar and was thus keenly opposed to any Western or capitalist influence. Instead he sought to encourage a pan-Arab identity and to this end he set in motion many conservative Islamic practices with *sharia* as the religious basis. Thus, people were banned from consuming alcohol and visiting nightclubs. Christian churches which had existed since many decades were ordered to be shut down. Arabic was now the only official language and to be used in government communication, road signs as well as all medium of instruction. People were asked to adopt the traditional Libyan dress and uphold Arab way of living.

Foreign Relations

Motivated by the ideology of pan-Arab nationalism, Gaddafi tried his best to establish a single Arab political entity that would extend North Africa and the Middle East. With this end in mind, he founded the Arab Revolutionary Front – while Sudan and Egypt joined promptly, in 1970 Syria declared its intention to come aboard. However, in the following years, Gaddafi's dream of Arab unification seemed to move further away from the reality. President Nasser's successor, Anwar Sadat initially advocated a political federation of Arab states instead of a unified Arab state. Later even this appeared improbable – September 1973 was decided as a deadline for implementing the Federation but the month came and went with none of the countries being able to agree on the specifics of the proposal.

On the international front, Gaddafi adopted a strong anti-Western and anti-capitalist stance from the beginning. Though initially the US sought to maintain a working relationship with the RCC – partly in order to ensure oil supplies and partly to maintain some strategic influence in the region – very soon the former realized that Libya was in no mood to relent. In 1970, soon after coming to power, the RCC ordered the US and Britain to remove all their military bases from Libyan soil. Also members of the native Italian and Jewish communities were asked to leave the country from 1970 onwards while all Italian-owned assets were seized by the Libyan government.

In order to offset Western capitalist influence, Libya began to purchase arms from France and Soviet Union, thus further heightening relations between the two superpowers who were already engaged in a Cold War around this time.

Over the years, Gaddafi developed a reputation for supporting radical, armed political groups from across the world. The Palestinian cause was one of his favourites since he considered the creation of the Israeli state in 1948, an act of high-handedness by Western powers. In order to equip the Arab states to wage 'continuous war' against Israel, Gaddafi announced a Jihad Fund in 1970 to finance anti-Israeli militants. Two years later, he created the First Nasserite Volunteers Centre to train guerrillas who would wage war against Israeli forces.

He was however often at loggerheads with PLO leader Yaseer Arafat, whom he thought unduly tame and instead supported radical anti-Israeli groups like Popular Front for the Liberation of Palestine, the Abu Nidal Organization, the Democratic Front for the Liberation of Palestine, the Palestinian Popular Struggle Front and As-Sa'iqa. One of the most high-profile cases was the massacre of Israeli athletes on their way to participate in the 1972 Munich Olympics by a militia group known as the Black September Group which was not only funded by Gaddafi but whose slain militants were brought to Libya and given a heroes' burial.

Apart from pro-Palestinian groups, Gaddafi funded or supported many other radical groups who according to him were fighting against Western capitalism and neo-colonialism. Among these were the Black Panther Party, Nation of Islam, Tupamaros, 19th of April Movement and National Liberation Front in the Americas, those like ANC in Africa, the Provisional Irish Republican Army, Action directe, ETA, the Red Brigades and the Red Army Faction in Europe as well as the Armenian Secret Army, Japanese Red Army, Free Aceh Movement and Moro National Liberation Front in Asia.

Gaddafi's support, direct or indirect, of so many militant groups raised the hackles of Western countries, especially United States. In April 1986, thus US warplanes based in Britain carried out bombing of several sites in Libya. In these raids, several members of Gaddafi's family were killed or injured and the Libyan leader himself escaped narrowly.

In 1988, the destruction of a civil aircraft over Lockerbie, Scotland shocked the world and Gaddafi was accused for his role in it. Both United Nations and the United States slapped sanctions on Libya which were lifted only in late 1990s, when the Libyan dictator agreed to hand over the alleged bombers to international authorities.

Though Gaddafi wanted to be known internationally as the leader of Third world fight against Western hegemony and neo-colonialism, according to critics, he was often inconsistent in his causes as well as oblivious to the brutal methods employed by the militant groups he supported. In the later years of 1990s, Gaddafi to some extent fell in line with UN expectations which paved the way Libya's acceptance into the international community.

Last Years

The early part of 2011 saw a wave of anti-government protests in many Middle Eastern and North African countries. Popularly known as the Arab Spring, it led to the deposition of Hosni Mubarak in Egypt as well as Zine al-Abidine Ben Ali in Tunisia. Very soon, the protests spread to Libya too and there began popular uprisings against the four-decade old dictatorship of Gaddafi.

The Libyan dictator tried his best to crush the uprisings by directing police fire and mercenary attacks at the protestors. The most brutal force was used against the rebels including heavy weaponry such as artillery, fighter jets and even helicopter gunships. With forces belonging both to Gaddafi and the opposition locked in conflict, on March 17 the UN Security Council authorized military intervention for the sake of civilians. By now Gaddafi's hold on power was appearing increasingly weak and late March two senior Libyan officials, Moussa Koussa and Ali Abdussalam el-Treki, defected to the side of the opposition.

However, it would still be August 2011 before rebel forces could enter Tripoli and seize most areas of the city.

Gaddafi managed to escape this time too but was later found and killed in Surt on October 20, 2011 as rebel forces took control of one of the last remaining Gaddafi's strongholds.

Legacy

Like most dictatorships, Gaddafi's reign too has been associated with the large-scale human rights abuses. During the 1970s, all potential political opposition was put down with brute force. This was a time when televised public hangings and mutilations of political opponents became a regular occurrence. In the next decade, Libyan authorities put in motion a policy of extrajudicial executions of political opponents in exile. Termed 'stray dogs,' these political rivals living abroad were hunted down and killed by Libyan secret agents. An attempted assassination of Gaddafi in May 1984, apparently facilitated by exiled Libyans and their domestic supporters, brought out the worst of his repressive measures. Overnight thousands of people were imprisoned and there remained no record of how many were killed by the authorities. But the bloodiest episode of political repression perhaps ever occurred on June 28 and 29, 1996 when more than 1,000 prisoners were shot dead by the security forces in Abu Salim prison, according to a report by Human Rights Watch.

Later the Libyan leader did not even spare civilians who had no any political agenda. In one of the more recent episodes of this kind of repression, in 2000 Gaddafi's government allowed widespread attacks on thousands of migrant African workers in Tripoli and Zawiyah, which left hundreds dead.

Among the most oft-reported aspects of Gaddafi's rule, at least in the foreign media, was his eccentric lifestyle. The Libyan leader was known to boast of a forty-member team of well-trained female bodyguards who were apparently all required to be virgins too. Another well-known media anecdote about Gaddafi was the "bulletproof tent" which served as his living quarters when he visited any foreign country. This tent was reportedly so heavy that it had to be flown in a separate plane. Again Gaddafi sported an unusual dressing style – at international conferences, Gaddafi would be seen in white flowing robes or ornate military uniforms. Even when he wore safari suits, they would be heavily embellished with traditional African patterns. Though seemingly bizarre, such accessories helped Gaddafi cultivate a personality cult, especially one that was based on an image of a true Bedouin and hence the true leader of Arabian and North African people.

On the positive side, Gaddafi perhaps more than any other African leader worked for the creation of African Union in 2002. He organized several meetings of African heads of state and especially persuaded Nigeria and South Africa to take a more active part in the formation of a federal body. Though much of this drive for a pan-African body was centred in his own delusions of grandeur – as witnessed in the 2008 Kings of Kings ceremony which was attended no less than 200 African leaders – it is true Gaddafi's enthusiasm for a United States of Africa brought at least some of the issues plaguing the continent into focus. □

Robert Mugabe

D.O.B. – 21st Feb., 1924 Country – Zimbabwe

Robert Mugabe is the President of Zimbabwe who has held complete sway over the country since 1980 when it became independent of colonial British rule. Though Mugabe started out as the leader of a democratically elected government. Over the years of his reign he used brutal force to wipe out all political opposition. Mugabe has also been held responsible for the economic collapse of Zimbabwe through his takeover of British-owned farms as well as widespread corruption. The national elections of 2009 in which he claimed victory was further criticized for irregularities and after a lot of popular pressure, Mugabe agreed to share power with opposition party, Movement for Democratic Change.

Early Life

Robert Gabriel Mugabe was born February 21, 1924, in Jesuit Mission outpost called Katuma. He came from a humble background with his father, Gabriel Matibili, working as a carpenter in a part of Africa known then as Nyasaland while his mother Bona, came from the Shona tribe.

In 1945, Mugabe passed out from Katuma's St. Francis Xavier College with a certificate in teaching. Thereafter, he worked as a teacher for at least fifteen years in Rhodesia and Ghana. Around this time, he also managed to go for higher education at Fort Hare University in South Africa. While staying in Ghana, he met Sally Hayfron who would go on to be his first wife.

Political Involvement

In 1960, Mugabe returned to Rhodesia and became interested in the freedom movement against the British colonizers. At that time, the nationalist movement was mainly led by the National Democratic Party, which Mugabe joined, even becoming its publicity secretary. In 1961, the colonial government banned NDP which however was put together again as the Zimbabwe African Peoples Union (ZAPU), under the initiative of prominent political leader Joshua Nkomo.

However, in 1963, Mugabe left ZAPU and started working in support of Reverend Ndabaningi Sithole to form the Zimbabwe African National Union (ZANU), a breakaway faction of ZAPU. Next year, Mugabe was arrested on charges of giving a subversive speech and was sentenced to ten years in prison. Mugabe used the time of his incarceration well – teaching English to his fellow-inmates, acquiring law degrees through correspondence courses and keeping himself aware of all the changes in the political landscape of his country. Incredibly enough, Mugabe even organized a coup from behind prison walls which ended with the deposition of Sithole as the leader of ZANU.

In the meantime in 1965, the prime minster of then Zimbabwe, Ian Smith announced a Unilateral Declaration of Independence according to which Rhodesia would be governed by white rulers. This went against Britain's plans of handing over the rule of Rhodesia to its own people and Smith's announced was condemned in the international stage.

Towards the end of 1974, Mugabe was released from prison and he immediately took charge of the anti-colonial movement in the country. At that time, the country was in the grip of a civil war between the black majority people and a white-ruled Rhodesian government that was led by Prime Minster Ian Smith. Mugabe rallied all nationalist political parties and brought them under a common umbrella which was named the Popular Front or the PF. To bring this about Mugabe joined hands with his erstwhile colleague, Nkmoko while Sithole was cast off to political oblivion. In this way, he managed to solidify his own political position in the country.

But as there was still some danger to his life and plans, Mugabe went into exile in Zambia and Mozambique. This helped him later to carry out guerilla attacks against the Rhodesian government from bases in nearby basis in Zambia, Angola and Mozambique. At the same time, he read up on Marxist and Maoist views and was heavily influenced by them. He also looked for allies in Asia and Eastern Europe from whom he could receive arms and training. Over all, he was careful to maintain good relations with Western countries who might be relied upon to make huge donations to Zimbabwe.

Eventually, compelled by his rising popularity at home and abroad, the British government invited Mugabe for talks in London in 1979 and this turned to be the most important meeting for the future of the country. This was known as the Lancaster House Agreement, which brought the major parties together so that they could agree on majority rule by the blacks while also promising to protect the rights and property of the white minority. The colonial government agreed to hold the first truly parliamentary elections under its administration in February 1980. Mugabe's party was now known as the ZANU-PF, or Zimbabwe African National Union and Popular Front. This way Mugabe ensured a massive scale of victory for himself and other black parties. In 1981, he became the Prime Minister of his country. Shortly after becoming the Prime Minster, Mugabe assured the 200,000 strong white minority including 4,500 commercial farmers that no harm would come to their lives and property.

Though Mugabe had come to power on the strength of democratic elections, he still suffered from political insecurity. In 1982, unrest broke out in the Matabeleland region of Zimbabwe, which was also a stronghold of ZAPU activists. Mugabe sent the Fifth Brigade of his army to quell the dissent and this North Korean-trained unit became infamous for its use of excessive force to subdue the insurgents. For the next five years, no less than 20,000 Ndebele civilians were massacred so that all political opposition was wiped out and Mugabe's claim to power could never be challenged from this part of the country again.

In 1987, however Mugabe changed tracks and reached out to the ZAPU, inviting it to merge with his ruling party, the ZANU-PF. This resulted in the creation of a single party regime where there was no effective opposition party. Robert Mugabe was now the head of an authoritarian state and as President held absolute power.

Growing Unrest

In 1990, a multi-party election was ostensibly held in Zimbabwe but which was actually marked by violence and serious irregularities. As predicted, Mugabe was re-elected President this time as well and he used this opportunity to further intimidate his political opponents.

During the early years of the 1990s, the Mugabe regime was facing increasing opposition from all over Zimbabwe. There were several causes for this, the primary among them being a sinking economy which was further burdened by Mugabe's support of President Laurent Kabila of the Democratic Republic of the Congo in his fight against rebels. Strikes broke out across the country and the nation-wide unrest still increased when in November 1998 Mugabe announced that he and members of his cabinet would receive pay increases.

There had always been factions within the ZANU-PF waiting for a chance to present a credible opposition to Mugabe. Now that initiative was taken up by trade union leader Morgan Tsvangirai who formed the Movement for Democratic Change or MDC in September 1999. In the national elections of 2000, the MDC won at least half of the seats for the parliament but the programme of intimidation and violence carried out on Mugabe's orders proved strong enough to prevent a change of government. Consequently, ZANU-PF and Mugabe continued to remain in control.

In 1992, Mugabe lost his wife to kidney disease. Four years later, on 17 August 1996, Mugabe married his former secretary, Grace Marufu, who was more than forty years younger to him and with whom he already had two children.

Economic Turmoil

In the meantime, the soldiers who had fought for ZANU-PF had started demanding their pound of flesh from the Mugabe regime. In desperation, they started taking over farms and other property owned by white people, with the implicit approval of the Mugabe government. This further heightened tension in the country and raised concern in the international community with Western powers like Britain demanding that Mugabe take measures to protect the white minority.

After Mugabe was re-elected in 2002 as the President of Zimbabwe, his policies became more openly oppressive. Mugabe ordered the confiscation of white-owned farms and in the process more than half of the country's white farmers were forced to give up their lands and property. Far from benefiting the ordinary black farmers of the country, the forced confiscation was tailored to benefit politically-connected individuals.

The biggest victim of such policies of Mugabe was the economy of Zimbabwe. Without experienced local farmers in place, the vacuum created by the forced confiscation of white-owned property meant disaster for the agricultural and trade sector. There was a marked shortfall of harvest and this together with natural calamities like droughts led to severe food shortage in the country. This was followed by another highly controversial step in which Mugabe ordered the razing of thousands of homes on charges that they were illegal structures. The consequence of a series of bad economic policies was that Zimbabwe was staring at financial ruin. In the latter half of 2000s, the country had the highest rate of inflation in the world and one of the highest rates of unemployment. In fact, in the months leading up to the 2008 elections, Zimbabwe had an inflation rate that shot above even 100,000 percent. An overwhelming majority of population did not have access to food, drinking water and fuel.

As Zimbabwe sank into a spiral of violence and suffering, Mugabe's popularity among his countrymen seemed to take a beating. But instead of taking steps to redress the situation, the dictator lashed out with further repressive measures. The press was banned from reporting facts and any voice of opposition was brutally silenced.

2008 Elections and Consequences

Despite being condemned internationally for the wave of suffering and oppression Mugabe had been unleashed in his country, he was still chosen by his party the ZANU-PF as its presidential candidate for the 2008 elections. However, some voices of opposition could now be heard against Mugabe's continuing misrule. While the MDC, appointed Tsvangirai as its presidential candidate, former finance minister and senior ZANU-PF leader Simba Makoni announced that he would be contesting the elections for the office of the president.

Elections were held for several levels – presidential, parliamentary and local. However, the slow, uncertain pace of release of results raised the suspicion that Mugabe was using to unfair means to show ZAN-PF the victorious party. The MDC released its own account of the results which showed that Mugabe had lost to Tsvangirai on account of obtaining somewhat less than half the votes. However, these results were dismissed by the government and after many days of confusion, it was announced that a run-off election would be held since no single candidate had secured an absolute majority.

The months leading to the repeat election were full of violence. Both the ruling ZANU-PF as well as opposing MDC claimed that the other was using the politics of intimidation and brute force against their supporters. Instead of bringing law and order under control, Mugabe heightened the air of suspicion and threat by passing several reactionary measures. Several MDC leaders like Tsvangirai as well as their supporters were detained by the Mugabe government who also took into custody diplomats from the US and UK who were stationed in Zimbabwe to report on the fairness of elections. Mugabe went so far as to suspend all humanitarian activities in the country and strongly implied in his speeches that even if he lost in the run-off elections, he would not hand over power.

Amidst this context of threat and violence, Tsvangirai announced that his party was withdrawing from the elections since there was no possibility of their being held in a free, impartial manner. The elections were still conducted and Mugabe was declared the winner even though both domestic opposition and international observers accused the Mugabe regime of engineering the results.

Agreement to Share Power

Though Mugabe had bulldozed his way to the Presidential office again, the international community began bearing down on the dictator to enter a power-sharing arrangement with the main opposition. The African nations in particular created enough pressure on Mugabe so as to force him to agree to a meeting organized by the Southern African Development Community and led by the South African Thabo Mbeki. At this meeting apart from Mugabe, Tsvangirai, and Arthur Mutambara, leader of a MDC breakaway group, would be present and ways would be found to bring about a better balance of political power in Zimbabwe.

Finally, on September 15, 2008, the three Zimbabwean leaders agreed on a comprehensive power-sharing arrangement. This came to be known as the Global Political Agreement according to which, Mugabe would continue to be the President of Zimbabwe but the MDC leader Tsvangirai would exercise some powers and act as the Prime Minister just as Mutambara would serve as a Deputy Prime Minister.

However, because of continuing friction between Mugabe and Tsvangirai over allocation of ministries and authority, the power-sharing agreement has proved to be a fragile one. After months of mutual accusations, the two parties managed to agree on the final draft of a new constitution. A referendum on March 2013 approved the constitution which was then signed into law by Mugabe in May 2013.

The most recent elections to be held in Zimbabwe were in July 2013. This too was conducted amidst accusations by MDC and Tsvangirai that large-scale irregularities and intimidation were perpetrated by Mugabe's forces and as such there was no chance of free and fair election results. Even the Constitutional Court put its seal of approval on the election results on the basis of Mugabe was re-elected as President of Zimbabwe on August 22, 2013.

Even at 90 years of age, Mugabe shows no sign of stopping and in August 2014, he was appointed the chairperson of the Southern African Development Community.

Legacy

Robert Mugabe continues as the President of Zimbabwe, though his days of absolute authority appear to be over. He remains one of the longest running heads of state in the world, having been in power since 1980 when Zimbabwe won independence from colonial British rule. His three and a half decade long reign has widely been criticized for political repression, mass murders and the complete ruin of the economy. While Mugabe still managed to hold on to power in the 2013 elections, there has been some realization on his part that he would have to acknowledge the aspirations of his people if his rule is to claim any legitimacy at all.

□

Jorge Rafael Videla

D.O.B. – 2nd August, 1925 Country – Argentine
D.O.D. – 17th May, 2013

Introduction

Jorge Rafael Videla (2 August 1925 – 17 May 2013) was a senior commander in the Argentine Army and President of Argentina from 1976 to 1981.

He came to power in a coup d'état that deposed Isabel Martínez de Perón. Two years after the return of a representative democratic government in 1983, he was prosecuted in the Trial of the Juntas for large-scale human rights abuses and crimes against humanity that took place under his rule, including kidnappings or forced disappearance, widespread torture and extra judicial murder of activists, political opponents as well as their families, at secret concentration camps. An estimated 13,000 - 30,000 political dissident vanished during this period. Videla was also convicted of the theft of many babies born during the captivity of their mothers at the illegal detention centres and passing them on for illegal adoption by associates of the regime. In his defence, Videla maintains the female guerrilla detainees allowed themselves to fall pregnant in the belief they wouldn't be tortured or executed. On 5 July 2010, Videla took full responsibility for his army's actions during his rule. "I accept the responsibility as the highest military authority during the internal war. My subordinates followed my orders," he told an Argentine court. Videla also sheltered many Nazi fugitives along with Juan Perón before him, Alfredo Stroessner of Paraguay and Hugo Banzer of Bolivia. He was under house arrest until 10 October 2008, when he was sent to a military prison.

Following a new trial, on 22 December 2010, Videla was sentenced to life in a civilian prison for the deaths of 31 prisoners following his coup. On 5 July 2012, Videla was sentenced to 50 years in prison for the systematic kidnapping of children during his tenure. The following year, Videla died in the Marcos Paz civilian prison five days after suffering a fall in a shower.

Early Life

Jorge Rafael Videla was born on 2 August 1925 in the city of Mercedes. He was the third of five sons born to Colonel Rafael Eugenio Videla Bengolea (1888–1952) and María Olga Redondo Ojea (1897–1987) and was christened in honor of his two older twin brothers, who had died of measles in 1923. Videla's family was a prominent one in San Luis Province, and many of his ancestors had held high public offices. His grandfather Jacinto had been governor of San Luis between 1891 and 1893, and his great-great-grandfather Blas Videla had fought in the Spanish American wars of independence and had later been a leader of the Unitarian Party in San Luis.

On April 7, 1948, Jorge Videla married Alicia Raquel Hartridge (born on September 28, 1927) daughter of Samuel Alejandro Hartridge Parkes (1890-1967), an English Argentine professor of physics and Argentine ambassador to Turkey, and María Isabel Lacoste Álvarez (1894-1939). They had seven children: María Cristina (1949), Jorge Horacio (1950), Alejandro Eugenio (1951–1971), María Isabel (1958), Pedro Ignacio (1966), Fernando Gabriel (1961) and Rafael Patricio (1953). Two of these, Rafael Patricio and Fernando Gabriel, joined the Argentine Army.

Army Career

Videla joined the National Military College (Colegio Militar de la Nación) on 3 March 1942 and graduated on 21 December 1944 with the rank of second lieutenant. After steady promotion as a junior officer in the infantry, he attended the War College between 1952 and 1954 and graduated as a qualified staff officer. Videla served at the Ministry of Defence from 1958 to 1960 and thereafter he directed the Military Academy until 1962. In 1971, he was promoted to brigadier general and appointed by Alejandro Agustin Lanusse as Director of the National Military College. In late 1973 the head of the Army, Leandro Anaya, appointed Videla as the Chief of Staff of the Army. During July and August 1975, Videla was the Head of the Joint Chiefs of Staff (Estado Mayor Conjunto) of the Argentine Armed Forces. In August 1975, the President, Isabel Perón, appointed Videla to the Army's senior position, the General Commander of the Army.

Upon the death of President Juan Perón, his widow and Vice President Isabel became President. Videla headed a military coup which deposed her on 24 March 1976, during increasing violence, social unrest and economic problems. A military junta was formed, made up of him, representing the Army; Admiral Emilio Massera representing the Navy; and Brigadier General Orlando Ramón Agosti representing the Air Force. Two days after the coup, Videla formally assumed the post of President of Argentina.

Human Rights Violations: Dirty War

The military junta is remembered for the forced disappearances of large numbers of students. The military junta took power during a period of terrorist attacks from the Marxist groups ERP, the Montoneros, FAL, FAR and FAP, who had gone underground after Juan Perón's death in July 1974, and violent right-wing kidnappings, tortures and assassinations from the Argentine Anticommunist Alliance, led by José López Rega, Perón's Minister of Social Welfare, and other death squads. The Baltimore Sun reported at the beginning of 1976 that "In the jungle-covered mountains of Tucuman, long known as 'Argentina's garden', Argentines are fighting Argentines in a Vietnam-style civil war. So far, the outcome is in doubt. But there is no doubt about the seriousness of the combat, which involves 2,000 or so leftist guerrillas and perhaps as many as 10,000 soldiers."

In late 1974 the ERP set up a rural front in Tucumán province and the Argentine Army deployed its 5th Mountain Brigade in counter insurgency operations in the province. In early 1976, the mountain brigade was reinforced in the form of the 4th Airborne Infantry Brigade that had until then been withheld guarding strategic points in the city of Córdoba against ERP guerrillas and militants.

The members of the junta took advantage of the guerrilla threat to authorize the coup and naming the period in government as the "National Reorganization Process". In all, 293 servicemen and policemen were killed in left-wing terrorist incidents in 1975 and 1976. Videla narrowly escaped three assassinations attempts by the Montoneros and ERP between February 1976 and April 1977.

Justice Minister Ricardo Gil Lavedra, who formed part of the 1985 tribunal judging the military crimes committed during the Dirty War, later declared, "I sincerely believe that the majority of the victims of the illegal repression were guerrilla militants". Some 10,000 of the disappeared were guerrillas of the Montoneros (MPM), and the People's Revolutionary Army (ERP).

According to human right groups, thousands of Argentines — perhaps as many as 15,000 or even 30,000— 'disappeared' while in the custody of the police or the military. 10,000 to 12,000 of the "disappeared," PEN (Poder Ejecutivo Nacional) detainees held in clandestine detention camps throughout the dictatorship, were eventually released under diplomatic pressure. Terence Roehrig, who wrote 'The prosecution of former military leaders in newly democratic nations': The cases of Argentina, Greece, and South Korea (McFarland & Company, 2001) estimates that of the disappeared "at least 10,000 were involved in various ways with the guerrillas". In the book Disposición Final by Argentine journalist Ceferino Reato, Videla confirms for the first time that between 1976 and 1983, 8,000 Argentinians have been murdered by his regime. The bodies were hidden or destroyed to prevent protests at home and abroad. Videla also maintained that female guerrilla detainees allowed themselves to become pregnant in the belief they wouldn't be tortured or executed, but they were. The children whom they bore in prison were taken from them, illegally adopted by military families of the regime, and their identities were hidden for decades.

Some 11,000 Argentines have applied for and received up to US$ 200,000 as monetary compensation from the state for the loss of loved ones during the military dictatorship. The Asambleapor los Derechos Humanos (APDH or Assembly for Human Rights) believes that 12,261 people were killed or disappeared during the 'National Reorganization Process'. Politically, all legislative power was concentrated in the hands of Videla's nine-man junta, and every important position in the national government was filled with loyal military officers.

Conflict with Chile: Beagle Conflict

During Videla's regime, Argentina rejected the binding Report and decision of the Court of Arbitration over the Beagle conflict at the southern tip of South America and started Operation Soberanía in order to invade the islands. In 1978, however, Pope John Paul II opened a mediation process. His representative, Antonio Samoré, successfully prevented full-scale war.

The conflict was not completely resolved until after Videla's time as president. Once the democratic rule was restored in 1983, the Treaty of Peace and Friendship of 1984 between Chile and Argentina (Tratado de Paz y Amistad), which acknowledged Chilean sovereignty over the islands, was signed and ratified by popular referendum.

Economic Policy

Videla largely left economic policies in the hands of Minister José Alfredo Martínez de Hoz, who adopted a free trade and deregulatory economic policy. During his tenure, the foreign debt increased fourfold, and disparities between the upper and lower classes became much more pronounced. The period ended in a tenfold devaluation and one of the worst financial crises in Argentine history.

Public Relations

One of Videla's greatest challenges was his image abroad. He attributed criticism over human rights to an anti-Argentine campaign. On 19 May 1976, Videla attended a luncheon with a group of Argentine intellectuals, including Ernesto Sábato, Jorge Luis Borges, Horacio Esteban Ratti (president of the Argentine Writers Society) and Father Leonardo Castellani. The latter expressed to Videla his concern regarding the disappearance of another writer, Haroldo Conti.

On 30 April 1977, Azucena Villaflor, along with 13 other women, started demonstrations on the Plaza de Mayo, in front of the Casa Rosada presidential palace, demanding to be told the whereabouts of their disappeared children. They became known as the Mothers of the Plaza de Mayo (Madres de Plaza de Mayo).

During a human rights investigation in September 1979, the Inter-American Commission on Human Rights denounced Videla's government, citing many disappearances and instances of abuse. In response, the junta hired the Burson-Marsteller ad agency to formulate a pithy comeback: Los argentinos somos derechos y humanos (Literally, "We Argentines are honest and humane") The slogan was printed on 250,000 bumper stickers and distributed to motorists throughout Buenos Aires to create the appearance of a spontaneous support of pro-junta sentiment, at a cost of approximately $16,117.

Videla used the 1978 FIFA World Cup for political purposes. He cited the enthusiasm of the Argentine fans for their victorious football team as evidence of his personal and the junta's popularity.

In 1980 Adolfo Pérez Esquivel, leader of the Peace and Justice Service (Servicio Paz y Justicia, SERPAJ) organization, was awarded the Nobel Peace Prize for reporting many of Argentina's human rights violations to the world at large.

Later Years

Videla relinquished power to Roberto Viola on 29 March 1981; the military regime continued until it collapsed after losing the Falklands war in 1982. Democracy was restored in 1983.

The new government began prosecution of top-ranking officers for crimes committed during the dictatorship in what was called the Trial of the Juntas of 1985. Videla was convicted of numerous homicides, kidnapping, torture, and many other crimes. He was sentenced to life imprisonment and was discharged from the military in 1985.

Videla was imprisoned for five years. In 1990, President Carlos Menem pardoned Videla and many other imprisoned former members of the military regime. Menem also pardoned the leftist guerrilla commanders accused of terrorism. In a televised address to the nation, President Menem said, "I have signed the decrees so we may begin to rebuild the country in peace, in liberty and in justice ... We come from long and cruel confrontations. There was a wound to heal.

Videla briefly returned to prison in 1998 when a judge found him guilty of the kidnapping of babies during the Dirty War, including the child of the desaparecida Silvia Quintela, and the disappearances of the commanders of the People's Revolutionary Army (ERP), Mario Roberto Santucho and Benito Urteaga. Videla spent 38 days in the old part of the Caseros Prison. Due to health issues, he was later transferred to house arrest.

In an August 2001, radio interview from exile in Spain, Mario Firmenich, the commander of the Montoneros guerrilla movement, said that, "In a country that experienced a civil war, everybody has blood in their hands."

Following the election of President Néstor Kirchner in 2003, there was a renewed widespread effort in Argentina to show the illegality of Videla's rule. The government no longer recognized Videla as having been a legal president of the country, and his portrait was removed from the military school. In 2003, Congress repealed the Ley de Punto Final, which had ended prosecutions for crimes under the dictatorship. In 2005, the Argentine Supreme Court ruled that the law had been unconstitutional. The government re-opened prosecution of crimes against humanity.

According to Argentina's Center for the Legal Study of Terrorism and its Victims, guerrilla groups also were implicated in the violence, killing or wounding some 13,000 Argentines before the coup d'état that established the military dictatorship. These were considered common rather than state crimes, and had exceeded the statute of limitation by the 21st century.

Death

On 17 May 2013, Videla was reported as having died of natural causes in his sleep while serving his sentence at a Marcos Paz prison. An autopsy revealed he died from multiple fractures and internal hemorrhaging caused by having slipped in a prison shower on May 12. According to a 2009 ruling by the military, he (and others) was convicted of human rights violations were not eligible for a military funeral. A private ceremony was held by his family.

Human rights organizations throughout the political compass denounced Videla, saying that he died without admitting what he was aware of the disappeared persons and kidnapped children. None of the tried ex-officers has provided details about the fate of those missing. Videla appeared mostly unrepentant for the actions against those whom he deemed terrorist subversives.

Several Argentine politicians commented on his death. Deputy Ricardo Gil Lavedra of the Radical Civic Union said that Videla will be remembered as a dictator, while Hermes Binner expressed condolences to the victims of his government. Hernán Lombardi, Minister of Culture of Buenos Aires city, praised Argentine democracy for having tried and sentenced the dictator. Ricardo Alfonsín said it was good that Videla had died in prison. Adolfo Pérez Esquivel, Argentine recipient of the 1980 Nobel Peace Prize, said, "The death of Videla should not delight anybody, we have to keep working for a better society, more just, more humane, so that all that horror never happens again".

Chief of the Cabinet of Ministers Juan Manuel Abal Medina, Jr. said that he was glad that, "Videla died prosecuted, sentenced and imprisoned in a common cell, repudiated by the Argentine people". At the time of Videla's death he was one of two surviving dictators of Argentina. His death leaves Argentina's last president during the dictatorship surviving: Reynaldo Bignone.

□

Conclusion

What is the relevance for dictatorships in this time and day?

With people no longer ready to be ruled on the strength of hereditary power and the call for right of self-determination rapidly getting louder in different parts of the world, it seems incredible that a sole individual can run a government that is the very anti-thesis of democracy.

But interestingly enough, it seems that even in these modern liberal times, democracy can be sidelined. And not only that, democracy can actually be used to gain power by a single party whose leader can then go on to rule with absolute authority, as happened in Adolf Hitler's Germany and Nicolai Ceausescu's Romania. What's more, such a dictator will then use his unquestioned power to change the very nature of the constitution to ensure that his dictatorship is legitimized and continued indefinitely.

Another less subtle variation of this is when a military leader takes advantage of political chaos and executes a coup. The bogey of foreign invasion or economic sanctions imposed on a country by international agencies is often used to justify a call for dictatorship, as happened in Iran and Iraq. All this is most common in societies where an earlier experiment with democracy has failed, like in many African nations, and the government has been too weak or corrupt to address the needs of the people.

Dictators have been common in communist countries because of the ideology of the supremacy of 'party' over anything else. Thus, the downfall of USSR and communism in its allied countries meant an end for many communist dictators. Even then some like North Korea continue to be ruled by dictators, who have established their own version of communism. On the other hand, though People's Republic of China still has a one-party political system, the entire government is not run by a single individual.

No matter what the mode of ascension to power, there are some features that are common to a dictatorship. The first of these is a personality cult – the leader who rises to power and ensures absolute authority over a government often uses a careful but relentless programme of self-aggrandizement. Propaganda about personal attributes of the dictator and the purported achievements of his rule are widely disseminated through official channels of communication. This in turn makes for another common feature of dictatorships, restrictions on media and press. In a dictatorship, print and electronic media are either pressured to carry out government-approved content or freedom of press banned outright. This way not only the truth about the present social, political, economic and cultural situation of a country is manipulated by a dictatorship but many times, even an imaginary past constructed with the aim of furthering the dictator's own power and rule.

All this is evidence of the complexity of the system of dictatorship – a fact that has helped it to evolve with changing political theories and practices and maintain its relevance to some extent.

And finally more often than not, a dictator leaves behind a negative or at least mixed legacy. The very nature of ascension of as well as continuation of power by a dictator necessitates use of force. Thus, a dictatorship is commonly associated with political repression, human rights abuse and in the worst instances, large-scale genocide – all of which are remembered with horror by victims and their successive generations.

And yet, there always exists certain sections of the population – whether in the home country or internationally – for whom a dictator is the answer to many problems of a government. The reasons for this are many – the promise of stability amidst warring factions in a government, the fear of foreign subjugation as well as the personal charisma of the dictator are all contributory factors in the perpetuation of the appeal of a dictatorship in today's world.

□□□